PHOTOSHOP CS

ROBERT SHUFFLEBOTHAM

BARNES
&NOBLE
BOOKS
NEW YORK

In easy steps is an imprint of Computer Step
Southfield Road . Southam
Warwickshire CV47 0FB . United Kingdom
www.ineasysteps.com

This edition published for Barnes & Noble Books, New York
FOR SALE IN THE USA ONLY
www.bn.com

Notice of Liability
Every effort has been made to ensure that this book contains
accurate and current information. However, Computer Step and the
author shall not be liable for any loss or damage suffered by readers
as a result of any information contained herein.

Trademarks
Photoshop® is a registered trademark of Adobe Systems
Incorporated. All other trademarks are acknowledged as belonging to
their respective companies.

Printed and bound in the United Kingdom

ISBN 0-7607-5826-3

Contents

Working with Type 133

10

Paths 143

11

Channels and Masks 153

12

Color Correction Techniques 163

13

Filters 175

14

Basic Theory

An understanding of the basics of color is important if you are to get the best out of Photoshop. Refer back to this section from time to time. As your understanding of Photoshop grows, so will your appreciation of the concepts of color that underpin the whole process of image capture and image manipulation.

This section also covers RGB, CMYK and monitor calibration.

Covers

Chapter One

Bitmaps and Vectors

Photoshop is an image-editing application with a wealth of tools and commands for working on digital images or bitmaps. There are utilities for retouching, color correcting, compositing and more. There are also over 90 functional and creative filters that can be applied to entire images, or selected areas within images.

A bitmap image consists of a rectangular grid, or raster, of pixels – in concept, very much like a mosaic. When you edit a bitmap you are editing the color values of individual pixels or groups of pixels.

Image-editing applications differ fundamentally from vector-based applications such as Adobe Illustrator and Macromedia FreeHand. In these applications, you work with objects that can be moved, scaled, transformed, stacked and deleted as individual or grouped objects, but all the time each exists as a complete, separate object.

These applications are called vector drawing packages, as each object is defined by a mathematical formula. Because of this, they are resolution-independent – you can scale vector drawings up or down (either in the originating application or in a page layout application such as QuarkXPress or Adobe InDesign) and they will still print smoothly and crisply.

You should always try to scan an image at, or slightly larger than, the size at which you intend to use it. This means you will avoid having to increase the size of the image.

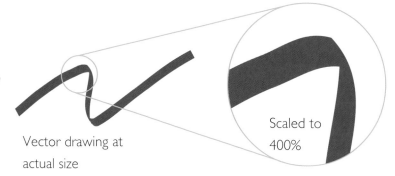

Vector drawing at actual size

Scaled to 400%

In contrast, bitmaps are created at a set resolution – a fixed number of pixels per inch. If you scan an image at a specific resolution, then double its size, you are effectively halving its resolution (unless you add more pixels). You are likely to end up with a blocky, jagged image, as you have increased the size of the individual pixels that make up the bitmap image.

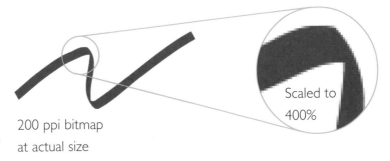

200 ppi bitmap
at actual size

Scaled to 400%

More, rather than less, color information is usually desirable, as this means the image can represent more shades of color, with finer transitions between colors and greater density of color, leading to a more realistic image.

Photoshop can handle images that use 16-bits per channel that originate from high-end digital cameras and scanners. 16-bit per channel images contain a far greater range of colors than 8-bit per channel images. The disadvantage of working with such images is that their file sizes are also dramatically larger. The bit depth per channel of an image appears in the title bar of the image window:

Waterfall(16bit).tif @ 66.7% (RGB/16)

Bitmaps and bit-depth

An important factor when the digital data for an image is captured, typically at the scanning stage, is its bit-depth. Bit-depth refers to the amount of digital storage space used to record information about the color of a pixel. The more bits you use, the more color information you can store to describe the color of a pixel – but also, the larger the file size you end up with.

To output realistic images using PostScript technology an image should be able to represent 256 gray levels. A 24-bit scan is sufficient for recording 256 gray levels for each of the Red, Green and Blue channels (8-bits for each channel), resulting in a possible combination of over 16 million colors.

Ideally, when you work on images in Photoshop you will do so using a 24-bit monitor capable of displaying over 16 million colors. This ensures that you see all the color detail in the image. Although you can work on images using only thousands of colors, for best results, especially where color reproduction is important, you need to work with as many colors as possible.

Pixels and Resolution

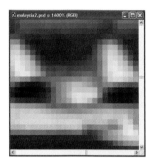

Pixels

A pixel is the smallest element in a bitmap image from a digital camera or a scanner. Pixel is short for "picture element". Zoom in on an image in Photoshop and you will start to see the individual pixels – the fundamental building blocks – that make up the image. When working in Photoshop, you are editing pixels, changing their color, shade and brightness.

Resolution

A key factor when working on bitmap images is resolution. This is measured in pixels per inch (ppi).

Pixels can vary in size. If you have an image with a resolution of 100 ppi, each pixel would be 1/100th of an inch square. In an image with a resolution of 300 ppi, each pixel would be 1/300th of an inch square – giving a much finer, less blocky result.

When working on images that will eventually be printed on a printing press, you need to work on high-resolution images. These are images whose resolution is twice the halftone screen frequency (measured in lines per inch – lpi) that will be used for final output – that is when you output to bromide, film, or directly to plate.

Printer resolution measured in dots per inch (dpi) is not the same as image resolution measured in pixels per inch (ppi). Printer dots are a fixed size, pixels can vary in size.

For example, for a final output screen frequency of 150 lpi – a typical screen frequency used for glossy magazines – you need to capture your image at a resolution of 300 ppi.

Resolutions of double the screen frequency are important for images with fine lines, repeating patterns or textures. You can achieve acceptable results, especially when printing at screen frequencies greater than 133 lpi, using resolutions of 1½ times the final screen frequency.

Images intended for multimedia presentations or the World Wide Web need only be 72 ppi, which is effectively the screen resolution.

To work with images for positional purposes only, as long as you can get accurate enough on-screen results and laser proofs, you can work with much lower resolutions.

RGB and CMYK Color Models

As you start working with Adobe Photoshop there are two color models that you need to be aware of. These are the RGB (Red, Green, Blue) and CMYK (Cyan, Magenta, Yellow and BlacK) color models.

RGB is important because it mirrors the way the human eye perceives color. It is the model used by scanners and digital cameras to capture color information in digital format, and it is the way that your computer monitor describes color.

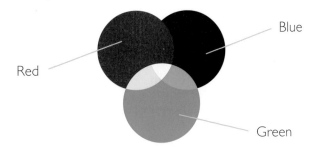

Red, green and blue are referred to as the "additive primaries". You can add varying proportions of the three colors to produce millions of different colors – but still a more limited range (or "gamut") than in nature, due to the limitations of the phosphor screen coating of the monitor. If you add 100% red, green and blue light together, you get white. You produce the "secondary" colors when you add red and blue to get magenta; green and blue to get cyan; red and green to get yellow.

The CMYK color model is referred to as the "subtractive" color model. It is important because this is the color model used by printing presses. If you subtract all cyan, magenta and yellow when printing you end up with the complete absence of color – white.

On the printing press, cyan, magenta, yellow and black are combined to simulate a huge variety of colors. Printers add black because, although in theory, if you combine 100% each of cyan, magenta and yellow you produce black, in reality, because of impurities in the dyes, you only get a muddy brown.

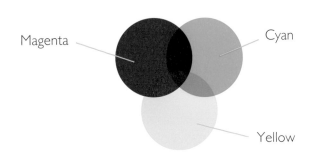

Color gamuts

Color gamut refers to the range of colors that a specific device is capable of producing. There are millions of colors in the visible spectrum that the eye can discern. Scanners, monitors and printing presses cannot reproduce every color in the visible spectrum – the range of colors they are capable of producing is their gamut.

From the desktop publishing point of view, the process of capturing digital color information, viewing and manipulating this on-screen and then finally printing the image using colored inks is complicated, because the gamut of a color monitor is different to the gamut of CMYK and PANTONE inks. There are colors (especially vibrant yellows and deep blues) that can be displayed on a monitor but cannot be printed using traditional CMYK inks.

When you convert from RGB to CMYK mode, Photoshop converts out-of-gamut colors (in this case, colors that can be seen on screen, but not printed) into their nearest printable equivalent.

Typically you will work in RGB mode if the image is intended for use on the World Wide Web or in a multimedia presentation. You can work in CMYK or RGB mode if the image is intended for print, but you must remember to convert to CMYK mode before saving/exporting in EPS or TIFF file format in order to use the image in a page layout application such as Adobe InDesign or QuarkXPress.

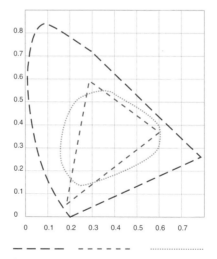

Visible Spectrum   Monitor   SWOP-CMYK

Color Management

No two devices that represent color, from scanner to monitor to printer, will reproduce color in exactly the same way. The aim of a color management system is to ensure, as far as possible, that the colors you see on your screen will be as close as possible to the colors you see in the finished work, whether in print or on screen.

Color management settings are available so that you can choose a color management workflow most suitable for your needs.

Using the Color Settings dialog box you can define how you manage color in your images as you work in Photoshop.

The very first time you launch Photoshop CS you will be prompted to choose your color management settings.

1 To specify color management settings for your Photoshop working environment, launch Photoshop, then choose Edit > Color settings (Command/Ctrl+Shift+K).

2 Choose the most appropriate setting for your intended final output from the Settings pop-up list. For example, if you are using Photoshop for images that will be used in multimedia presentations, or on the World Wide Web, choose Web Graphics Defaults. If you are working with images that will be color separated then printed using CMYK inks, choose Europe or US Prepress Defaults as appropriate.

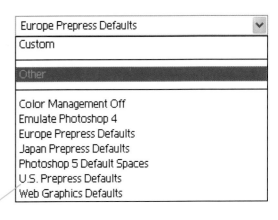

3 Leave the Advanced Mode option deselected unless you need to change one of the advanced settings.

4 Only make changes to the default settings when you have gained experience of using Photoshop and you have a valid reason for making changes, or if you have consulted with your commercial printer and they have suggested changes to suit your specific output requirements.

If you feel that you are not achieving good color in printed output, consult your commercial printer about creating custom settings for color management.

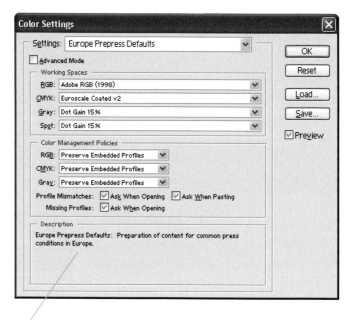

A CMS (Color Management System) is used to translate colors accurately from one color device to another. It attempts to represent a color consistently from the color space in which the image was created to the color space used at output, making adjustments so that color is displayed as consistently as possible across a range of monitors and other devices.

5 To get a better understanding of how the settings work in the Color Settings dialog box, roll your cursor over the pop-up lists. The Description area at the bottom of the palette updates with information on how the options affect the image.

Monitor Calibration

It is important to calibrate your monitor so that colors in your image are displayed accurately. Calibrating your monitor should eliminate any color casts (typically reddish or blueish) on your monitor and ensure that the monitor displays grays as neutrally as possible.

Use the Adobe Gamma utility to calibrate the monitor you are using and to define the RGB color space that your monitor can display. Once you have calibrated your monitor, Photoshop can compensate for the differences between the color space in which your image resides and the color space of the monitor you are using.

The Adobe Gamma utility enables you to calibrate the contrast and brightness, gamma (midtones), color balance and the white point of the monitor. Calibration settings that you create are saved as an ICC (International Color Consortium) profile with an .icm extension. Use the Adobe Gamma Wizard if you do not have previous experience of calibrating a monitor.

1 (Windows) Choose Control Panel from the Start Menu. Double-click the Adobe Gamma icon to display the dialog box.
(Macintosh) Use the Apple menu to choose Control Panel>Adobe Gamma. Choose Step by Step (Wizard), then click the Next button.

Hardware-based color calibration utilities are more accurate than the Adobe Gamma utility. You should use only one calibration utility. Colors may appear incorrectly if you use more than one utility.

2 Click the Load button to choose a monitor profile which matches the monitor you are using most closely.
(Windows) Profiles are stored in the Windows\System32\spool\drivers\color folder.
(Mac) Profiles are stored in the System/Library/ColorSync/Profiles folder.

Profiles should be available from your monitor manufacturer's website.

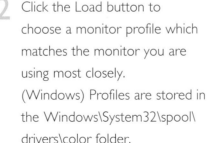

Leave your monitor turned on for at least 30 minutes before you calibrate.
This allows the phosphors time to warm up fully and the display to stabilize.

3 Adjust the Brightness and Contrast settings of your monitor. Refer to the monitor handbook if you are unsure of how to adjust these settings. Click the Next button.

4 Only change the Phosphors pop-up if you know that your monitor's phosphors are different from the default selection. Click the Next button.

Defocus your eyes slightly to help achieve the correct setting for the View Single Gamma slider.

5 With the View Single Gamma Only option selected, drag the Gamma slider until the square in the middle of the patterned lines fades, as far as possible, into the pattern. This defines the brightness of the midtones on your monitor. Click the Next button. For Desired Gamma choose a target gamma. This option is not available on Windows systems which cannot control the monitor. For images intended for the World Wide Web or multimedia presentations, choose a gamma of 2.2. If you intend to print images using CMYK inks, you should typically choose a gamma of 1.8. Click the Next button.

For monitor calibration to be effective, you should not adjust the brightness and contrast settings on your monitor after you have completed the calibration process, and you must ensure that the lighting conditions within the room remain constant.

6 Leave the Hardware White Point on the default setting unless you know this to be inaccurate. Click Next. Leave Adjusted White Point on Same as Hardware unless you want to view the image at a different color temperature to that set by the monitor's factory-specified setting. Click the Next button.

7 Click the Finish button to save settings as an .icm compatible profile. Name the profile and save it to the ColorSync Profiles folder.

The Working Environment

This section covers the basics of the Photoshop working environment, getting you used to the Photoshop window, the Toolbox, palettes and a number of standard Photoshop conventions that you will find useful as you develop your Photoshop skills.

It also covers the basics of printing composite images to a color inkjet printer as well as techniques for undoing commands as you work on your images.

Covers

Chapter Two

The Photoshop Screen Environment

There are three "screen modes" to choose from when working on images in Photoshop. The screen mode icons are located at the bottom of the toolbox. Full Screen with Menu Bar mode is useful when working on individual images because it clears away the clutter of the Finder environment (Mac) or the Windows desktop. Use Full Screen mode to see the image without the distraction of other screen elements, and without any other colors interfering with the colors in your image.

Standard Screen Mode

Full Screen with Menu Bar Mode

Full Screen Mode

Click this icon to return to Standard Screen Mode.

Click this icon to go to Full Screen with Menu Bar Mode.

Click this icon to go to Full Screen Mode. Press the Tab key to hide/show the Toolbox and palettes.

Click the Edit in ImageReady button to launch ImageReady. (See page 206).

Command (often referred to as "Apple" on the Mac) and Ctrl (Windows) – and Alt/option (Mac) and Alt (Windows) – are used identically as modifier keys. Shift is standard on both platforms.

This book uses Alt, with an uppercase "A", to denote both the Macintosh and Windows key of that name.

Windows environment

The Windows environment offers identical functionality to the Macintosh environment, as you can see from a comparison of the Windows and Macintosh screen shots.

Windows users can use the right mouse button to access context sensitive menus; Mac users can hold down the Control key and press their single mouse button.

The Image window

Every time you launch Photoshop the Welcome screen appears. Click on one of the listed links, or click the Close button to start working with Photoshop. To prevent the Welcome screen appearing the next time you launch Photoshop, deselect the Show this dialog at startup option.

Title bar

Close button

Image

Sizes Bar

Scroll bars

View %

Resize box

Using the Toolbox

There are a number of useful general techniques that relate to choosing tools in the Toolbox, including those from the expanded range of hidden tool pop-ups.

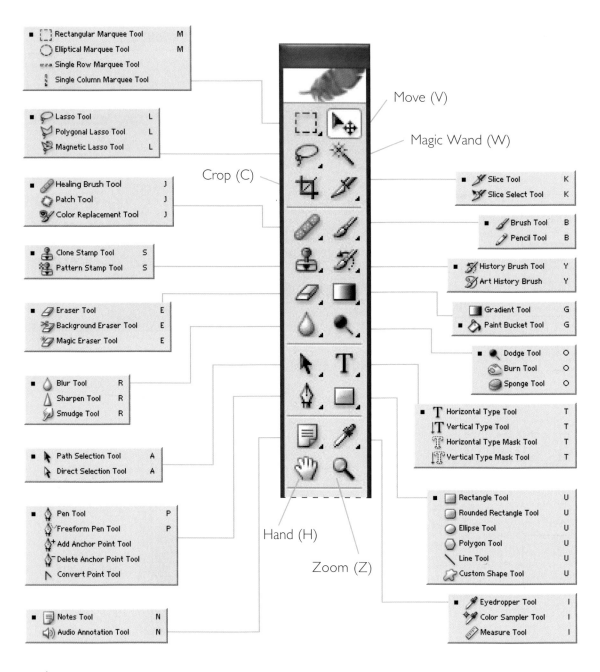

Rectangular Marquee Tool — M
Elliptical Marquee Tool — M
Single Row Marquee Tool
Single Column Marquee Tool

Lasso Tool — L
Polygonal Lasso Tool — L
Magnetic Lasso Tool — L

Healing Brush Tool — J
Patch Tool — J
Color Replacement Tool — J

Clone Stamp Tool — S
Pattern Stamp Tool — S

Eraser Tool — E
Background Eraser Tool — E
Magic Eraser Tool — E

Blur Tool — R
Sharpen Tool — R
Smudge Tool — R

Path Selection Tool — A
Direct Selection Tool — A

Pen Tool — P
Freeform Pen Tool — P
Add Anchor Point Tool
Delete Anchor Point Tool
Convert Point Tool

Notes Tool — N
Audio Annotation Tool — N

Move (V)
Magic Wand (W)
Crop (C)
Hand (H)
Zoom (Z)

Slice Tool — K
Slice Select Tool — K

Brush Tool — B
Pencil Tool — B

History Brush Tool — Y
Art History Brush — Y

Gradient Tool — G
Paint Bucket Tool — G

Dodge Tool — O
Burn Tool — O
Sponge Tool — O

Horizontal Type Tool — T
Vertical Type Tool — T
Horizontal Type Mask Tool — T
Vertical Type Mask Tool — T

Rectangle Tool — U
Rounded Rectangle Tool — U
Ellipse Tool — U
Polygon Tool — U
Line Tool — U
Custom Shape Tool — U

Eyedropper Tool — I
Color Sampler Tool — I
Measure Tool — I

...cont'd

Create your own, custom keyboard shortcuts using Edit>Keyboard Shortcuts. You can either edit the default shortcuts set, or create a new set by clicking the New button. Click on a command in the commands scroll list, enter a keyboard shortcut combination in the shortcut entry area that appears to the right, then click the Add Shortcut button. Click OK when you finish creating shortcuts.

Double-click on a tool to show the Options bar for that tool if it is not already showing.

When you select a tool in the Toolbox, the Options bar, extending across the top of the Photoshop window, updates according to the tool you select. Get into the habit of checking these settings before you proceed to use the tool.

Use Display & Cursor Preferences in the Edit> Preferences menu to change the default appearance of painting and other cursors.

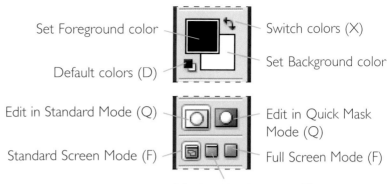

Set Foreground color — Switch colors (X)

Default colors (D) — Set Background color

Edit in Standard Mode (Q) — Edit in Quick Mask Mode (Q)

Standard Screen Mode (F) — Full Screen Mode (F)

Full Screen Mode with Menu Bar (F)

Edit in ImageReady

1 Press the keyboard shortcut (in brackets) to access tools.

2 Click and hold on any tool with a small triangle in the bottom right corner to see all tools in that tool group.

3 Hold down Alt/option and click on any tool in a tool group to cycle through the available tools. Alternatively, hold down Shift, then press the keyboard shortcut for that tool group a number of times. For example, press "O" three times to cycle through all the tools in the Dodge tool group.

4 Press Tab to hide/show all palettes, including the toolbox. Hold down Shift, then press the Tab key to hide/show all palettes except the Toolbox.

5 Press Caps Lock to change the painting or brush size cursor to a precise crosshair cursor, which indicates the center of the painting tool. Press Caps Lock again to return to the standard cursor display.

Document and Scratch Sizes

The Sizes Bar is useful for monitoring disk space and memory considerations as you work on your images.

Document Sizes

With Document Sizes selected, you will see two numbers separated by a slash. The first number is the size of the image when all layers are flattened. The second number may be larger and represents the file storage size whilst the image contains additional layers and/or alpha channels you may have set up. In images that consist of only a single layer, with no additional channels, both numbers are the same.

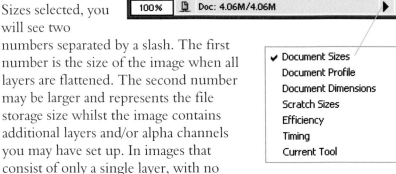

Use the Plug-ins & Scratch Disk preferences (Edit> Preferences> Plug-Ins & Scratch Disks) to specify the hard disk you want Photoshop to use as a Scratch disk. Ideally, the primary Scratch disk should be your fastest hard drive.

Scratch Sizes

The Scratch disk is an underlying technical detail that you should be aware of when using Photoshop. The Scratch disk is a designated hard disk that Photoshop utilizes as "virtual" memory if it runs out of memory (RAM) whilst working on one or more images.

To improve performance when working with large image files a Scratch disk should be on a different drive than the one where the image is located.

With Scratch Sizes selected in the Sizes Bar you again see two numbers separated by a slash. The first number represents the amount of memory (RAM) Photoshop needs to handle all currently open pictures. The second number represents the actual amount of memory available to Photoshop. When the first number is greater than the second, Photoshop is using the Scratch disk as virtual memory.

As a general rule of thumb when working in Photoshop, you should have free disk space of at least 3–5 times the file size of the image you are working on. This is because Photoshop makes use of the Scratch disk as virtual memory and because Photoshop needs to hold more than one copy of the image you are working on for the Undo, Revert and History palette functions.

Ruler Guides and Grids

You can show a grid in your image window to help with alignment and measuring, and you can also drag in ruler guides from the rulers. Both sets of guides are non-printing. Customize the appearance of the grid and guides using Edit>Preferences>Guides, Grid & Slices.

Make sure that Snap to Guides is selected in the View menu if you want cursors and selections to snap to guides and the grid. This is very useful for aligning elements accurately.

1 To hide or show the grid, choose View>Show/Hide Grid.

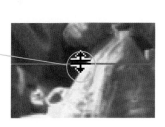

2 To create a ruler guide, first choose View>Show Rulers to display the rulers along the top and left edges of the image window. Position your cursor in a ruler and then click and drag onto your image to create either a vertical or horizontal guide.

Use keyboard shortcuts: Command/Ctrl+; to Hide/Show ruler guides; Command/Ctrl+' to Hide/Show the grid.

3 To reposition a ruler guide, select the Move tool, position your cursor on a guide, then click and drag. The cursor changes to a bi-directional arrow when you pick up a guide. To remove a ruler guide, drag the ruler guide back into the ruler it came from. Alternatively, choose View>Clear Guides to remove all guides.

Take care when repositioning ruler guides that you don't reposition an entire layer accidentally. Make sure you see the bi-directional arrows which indicate that you are dragging a guide.

4 To temporarily hide any grid or guides in order to preview the image without the clutter of non-printing guides, choose View> Extras (Command/Ctrl+H). Use the same command to bring back the guides and grid.

Moving Around

Use any combination of the Navigator palette, the Zoom tool, the Hand tool and the scroll bars for moving around and zooming in and out of your image.

1 Choose Window>Show Navigator to show the Navigator palette. In the palette, you can double-click the % entry box, enter a zoom % (0.20 – 1600%), then press Return/Enter. Alternatively, drag the zoom slider to the right to zoom in, or to the left to zoom out. Each time you change your zoom level, the view in the Preview area updates.

2 Drag the red View box in the Preview area to move quickly to different areas of your image.

3 To use the Zoom tool, select it, position your cursor on the image and click to zoom in on the area around your cursor, in preset increments. With the Zoom tool selected, hold down Alt/option. The cursor changes to the zoom out cursor; click to zoom out in the preset increments.

4 With the Zoom tool selected, you can also click and drag to define the area you want to zoom in on.

5 You can use the Hand tool in addition to using the scroll bars to move around your image when you have zoomed in on it. Select the tool, position your cursor on the image, then click and drag to reposition.

The Info Palette

The Info palette (Window>Info) provides useful numerical read-outs relative to the position of the cursor on your image.

You can use it as an on-screen densitometer to examine color values at the cursor. There are two color read-outs. As a default, the first color read-out is the actual color under the cursor. For example, a read-out of red, green, and blue color components in an RGB image. The default second read-out is for cyan, magenta, yellow and black values.

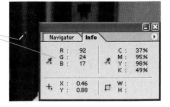

An exclamation mark next to the CMYK readouts indicates that a color is outside the printable CMYK gamut or range of colors.

The palette also displays x and y coordinates, giving the precise location of the cursor as it moves over the image.

If you create a selection, there is a read-out of the width and height of the selection. The palette also displays values for some options such as rotating, skewing and scaling selections.

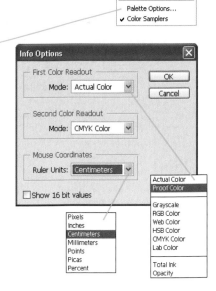

1   To change the default settings for the Info Palette, choose Palette Options from the Info palette menu.

2   Use the Mode pop-ups to choose the first and second color read-outs.

3   You can also choose a unit of measurement for mouse coordinates.

Palette Techniques

There are seventeen floating palettes in Photoshop, (not including the Toolbox or the Options bar). These movable palettes appear in front of images. Initially the palettes are grouped together.

1 You can show any of the palette groups by selecting the appropriate palette from the Window menu. To close a palette, click on the Close button (Mac) or Close icon (Windows) in the title bar of each palette.

This page uses Macintosh and Windows screen shots to illustrate the degree of similarity in functionality between the Windows and Macintosh platforms.

2 To move a palette, simply position your cursor in the title bar, then click and drag.

3 To choose a particular palette, click on the appropriate tab just below the title bar. You can drag these tabs to create separate palettes. Alternatively, you can drag a tab into another palette to create your own custom groupings of palettes.

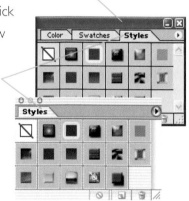

Choose Window> Workspace> Reset palette locations to recreate the default arrangement of Photoshop's palettes.

4 You can shrink or roll up palettes to make the most of your available screen space. Click the Zoom box (Mac) or Minimize icon (Windows) in the title bar of the palette. Repeat the procedure to restore the palette to its original size. (You have to click twice on the Zoom/Minimize icon if the palette has been resized.)

Double-click a palette tab to collapse the palette to its tab and title bar only. Double-click the tab again to restore it to its previous size.

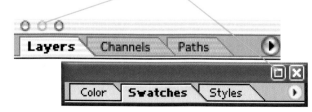

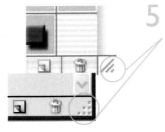

Press the Tab key to hide/show all palettes including the Toolbox. Hold down Shift, then press Tab to hide/show currently visible palettes, with the exception of the Toolbox.

5 Use standard Macintosh and Windows techniques to resize the Swatches, Navigator, Layers, Channels, Actions, Styles and Paths palettes by dragging.

6 With a painting or editing tool selected, to restore the default settings for all tools, click the drop-down triangle for the Tool Pop-up palette, then click the palette menu triangle. Choose Reset All Tools from the pop-up menu.

Reset Tool
Reset All Tools

For the Brush Preset picker, the Brushes palette and the Brush pop-up palette presets, you must click the drop-down triangle, then click the

pop-up menu triangle from within the palette.

7 All palettes have a palette menu for accessing a range of commands or options relevant to the palette. Click the triangle to access the palette menu.

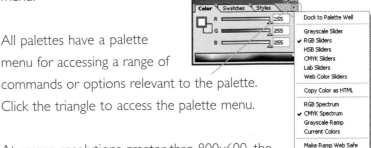

Choose Window> Workspace>Save Workspace to save the current position of your palettes. Enter a name for this workspace arrangement in the Save Workspace dialog box. Choose Window>Workspace then select the name of the workspace to reset palettes to this arrangement.

8 At screen resolutions greater than 800x600, the Options bar has a palette docking area on the right-hand side. Drag a palette tab into the docking area to create a drop-down palette. Click on the palette tab to access the palette. Click on the triangle in the palette tab to access the palette menu for the palette. After making changes to settings in a palette, it collapses back into the docking well when you perform another action on the image. Drag the palette out of the docking well to revert the palette to a standard floating palette.

Saving and Loading Custom Settings

When you save settings, you are creating an independent file which stores the custom information.

The Swatches, Styles and Actions palettes, the Brushes presets, along with dialog boxes such as Duotones, Levels and Curves, have Save and Load options which allow you to save custom settings made in the palette or dialog box and then load them into the same image, or into other Photoshop images, when required. The following example uses the Swatches palette.

1 After creating a custom Swatches palette (see Chapter 5), choose Save Swatches in the palette menu (in a dialog box, click the Save button).

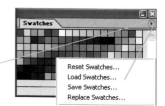

It's a good idea to set up a folder within your Adobe folder, or any other appropriate location, for saving your own custom settings. This means you will always be able to access and load the settings quickly and conveniently whenever you need them.

2 The Save dialog box prompts you for a file name and location in which to save the settings. The default Color Swatches folder is in the Presets folder within the Photoshop CS folder. The extension for a Color Swatches file is .aco. Make sure you save the file with the correct extension.

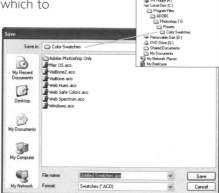

Look in the Presets folder, within the Photoshop CS folder, for brush presets that come with Photoshop. Try the Assorted Brushes folder as a starting point for experimenting with different brush types.

3 To load previously saved settings, choose Replace Swatches or Load Swatches in the palette menu (in a dialog box click the Load button), then specify the location of the settings you previously saved. Click on the name, then click Open. Load Swatches adds the new swatches to the existing swatches in the palette. Replace Swatches replaces the current swatches with the new set.

Choose Reset Swatches in the palette menu to restore settings to their original defaults.

Printing Composites – Mac

A composite image is an image which has not been color separated and can be useful for low-cost, basic proofing purposes. In a black-and-white laser printer composite, you get a complete image on one sheet of paper, with all color values converted to shades of gray.

The appearance of the Page Setup dialog box varies according to the printer selected. Non-PostScript printers do not offer a complete set of options.

1 Choose File>Page Setup. Select the printer you want to print to from the Format for pop-up menu. Set Paper Size and Orientation, and a Scale % if required. OK the dialog box.

2 Choose File>Print with Preview to see a representation of the image as it will print on the specified paper size.

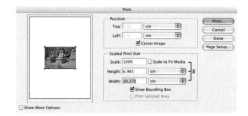

3 Click the Show More Options box, then choose Output from the drop down menu if you want to specify additional printed information such as Crop Marks and Calibration bars. As you switch on the various options they appear in the preview area.

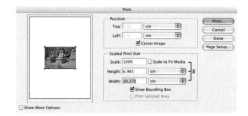
Binary encoding is a more compact and quicker format than ASCII for sending image information to a printer. You may need to choose ASCII if you are printing across a network.

4 Click the Screen button to change the size, angle and shape of the halftone screen dots. This can be useful for creating special effects. Click the Transfer button to map brightness values in an image to different shades when printed. Background and Border are useful when printing slides. Use Bleed to print outside the "imageable" area of the page when outputting to an imagesetter.

Printing Composites – Windows

A composite image is an image which has not been color separated and can be useful for low-cost, basic proofing purposes. In a black and white laser printer composite, you get a complete image, with all color values converted to shades of gray.

1 To print a composite proof, choose File>Page Setup. Select your paper size from the Size pop-up menu. Check that Orientation is correct. Click OK.

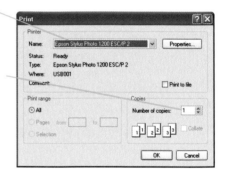

2 Choose File>Print. Make sure the correct printer is selected from the Name pop-up menu. Enter the number of copies you want to print. Some options are available only if you are printing to a PostScript printer.

3 Click the Properties button in the Print dialog box to set controls specific to your printer. Refer to the manufacturer's manuals for information on the options available for the printer. Click OK.

4 OK the Print dialog box.

Picture Package

The Picture Package command enables you to print multiple copies of an image, at various sizes, on a single sheet of paper.

1 To create a Picture Package, choose File>Automate>Picture Package. Select the image you want to use from the Use pop-up menu.

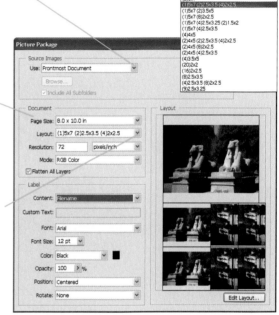

2 From the Document area, choose the page size you want to print onto. Then choose a layout arrangement from the Layout pop-up. The Layout area on the right updates to indicate the positioning of the images. Specify Resolution and Color Mode options.

Click the Edit Layout button in the bottom of the Layout area to manually arrange the images in your picture package:

3 Use the Content pop-up to choose a label if required. Select Custom Text to enter details in the Custom Text field. Control the appearance and position of text labels using the other controls.

4 When you OK the dialog box, Photoshop prepares the multiple copies of the image as a single picture package file that you can print or save.

The History Palette

Every time you modify your image this is recorded in the History palette as a history state. The History palette records the last 20 states of the image.

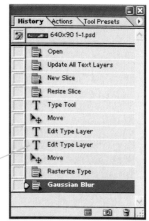

As soon as you close an image, all recorded history states and snapshots are discarded.

Use the History palette to return to a previous state of the image within the current work session. The most recent state of the image appears at the bottom of the list in the palette. Each state indicates the name of the tool or command used on the image.

1 To return to a previous state of the image, make sure that the History palette is showing.

You can still use Edit>Undo to undo the last operation. In effect this steps you back one state in the History palette.

2 Click on a state in the History palette. The image reverts to that stage of the work session. States after the state you click on are dimmed. These subsequent states will be discarded if you continue to work from the selected state.

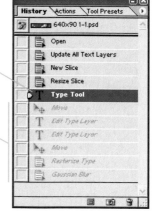

Use File>Revert to revert to the state of your image as it was when you last did a File>Save. The Revert command appears as a state in the History palette.

3 Alternatively, drag the state slider up or down to indicate the state you wish to move to. Or, choose Step Forward/Step Backward from the palette menu in the History palette, or from the Edit menu, to move sequentially through the states. You can also use the keyboard shortcuts Command/Ctrl+Shift+Z to move to the next state. Use Command/Ctrl+Alt/option+Z to move to the previous state.

Deleting, Clearing & Purging States

There are three essential techniques for controlling the states listed in the History palette.

Deleting states

You can delete states from the History palette to remove the changes to the image recorded by that state and all subsequent states.

Both techniques for deleting states delete the selected state and all states that occur after it. In other words, you are reverting to the state of the image previous to the state you delete.

1 To delete a history state, click on the name of the state, then choose Delete from the palette menu in the History palette.

| Dock to Palette Well |
| Step Forward |
| Step Backward |
| New Snapshot... |
| Delete |
| Clear History |
| New Document |
| History Options... |

2 Alternatively, drag the state into the Wastebasket icon at the bottom of the palette.

Clearing states

You can use Edit>Undo to cancel the Clear States command.

Clearing states leaves the image at its current state, but removes all previous states from the History palette.

1 To clear the History palette, use the palette menu to choose Clear History. All recorded states are deleted from the History palette, leaving the image at its most recent state.

Purging states

You cannot undo the Purge states commands.

Purging states is useful if you get a low memory message. This is typically because the Undo buffer is becoming full with the changes to the image that it is having to record. When you purge states they are deleted from the Undo buffer, freeing up memory.

Choose Edit> Preferences> General to change the number of history states recorded in the History palette. Enter the number of History states you want to record.

1 To purge states, hold down Alt/option, then choose Clear History from the palette menu in the History palette. This command purges history states from the active image.

2 Choose Edit>Purge Histories if you want to purge all history states for all open images.

Taking Snapshots

By default the History palette records the results of the last 20 operations performed on an image. Older states of the image are automatically deleted to keep memory free for Photoshop. You can keep particular states of an image during a work session by taking a "snapshot" of the image.

A snapshot is created by default when you open an image. This appears at the top of the History palette.

1 To create additional snapshots, click on any state in the History palette.

2 Choose New Snapshot from the palette menu in the History palette. In the New Snapshot dialog box enter a name. OK the dialog box. A new snapshot is added in the top section of the History palette.

Snapshots exist for the current work session only. When you close an image, all snapshots are lost.

3 Click on a snapshot to revert to the state of the image when the snapshot was created. If you select a snapshot, then continue to work on the image, all history states are lost.

4 To delete a snapshot, click once on the snapshot to select it, then click on the Wastebasket icon at the bottom of the palette.

5 To rename a snapshot, double-click the snapshot name. Enter a name for the snapshot, then click OK.

Opening and Saving Files

Adobe Photoshop began life with the primary purpose of converting image formats for use on different applications and platforms. Since then it has gone on to become a market-leading image-editing application. This chapter covers the basic techniques of opening and saving images in Photoshop.

Covers

Chapter Three

Opening Images in Photoshop

Once you have launched Photoshop you can open images using the File menu. Some specialist file formats open using the File> Import command.

1. To open a picture from within Photoshop, choose File>Open. This takes you into the Open dialog box. Navigate through folders and sub-folders as necessary to locate the file you wish to open, click on the file name to select it, then click Open. Alternatively, just double-click the file name.

Double-click Photoshop file icons in the Windows or Macintosh file-management environments to open the file. If Photoshop is not running, this will also launch Photoshop.

2. Select the Show All Readable Documents (Mac), or choose All Formats from the Files of type pop-up (Windows), to show all files in the selected folder.

3. You can also open recently opened files by choosing File>Open> Recent. Select a file from the list.

Choose Edit> Preferences>File Handling, then enter a number for Recent file list contains to control the number of files that appear in the Recent files sub-menu:

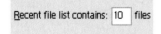

4. (Mac) To search for a file that you want to open from within the Open dialog box, click the Find button. Enter the file name, then click Find/ Find Again, until you find the file.

Scanning into Photoshop

You can scan into Photoshop either using the TWAIN interface, or using a scanner plug-in designed for use with Photoshop. If your scanner does not have a plug-in for Photoshop, you can use the scanner software to scan the image, save the image in TIFF, PICT or BMP format, then open the file in Photoshop.

Make sure the plug-in for your scanner is in Photoshop's Import/Export plug-ins folder. Plug-in modules for installed scanners appear in the File>Import sub-menu.

1   To create a scan from within Photoshop, choose File>Import, then select the appropriate device from the sub-menu, or;

2   Choose File>Import>Twain_32. This takes you into your scanning software.

The first time you scan into Photoshop or ImageReady using the TWAIN interface, or when you want to change the image capture device, choose File>Import> TWAIN Select. Select the appropriate icon for your scanner or digital camera, and click OK to specify the device.

Refer to your scanning software manual for details of the controls available. Typically, you can choose settings for scan mode (grayscale, color, line art etc.), resolution, scale, contrast, brightness and gamma settings.

Many of the scanning controls have equivalent functions in Photoshop. Scanning options vary from scanner to scanner, but you should be able to specify whether you are scanning a transparency or a photograph. The other essential decisions you need to make at this stage are mode, resolution and scale. You will also need to specify a crop area in the preview window.

3   Click the Scan button. Wait until the scanning process finishes and the image appears in an untitled Photoshop window. Save the image.

Opening Photo CD Images

Photo CD files are found inside the Images folder within the Photo CD folder.

The Photo CD format, developed by Kodak, is a popular method for creating and storing digital images, providing an extremely broad range of color. The Kodak Precision Color Management System (KPCMS) lets you control the color mode and display of Photo CD images by specifying profiles for the source film and the destination output device.

The Kodak Precision Color Management System is automatically installed on your system when you install Photoshop.

1 To open a Photo CD image, choose File>Open. Select the image you want to open and click OK. Use the Pixel Size pop-up menu to choose a resolution from 128 × 192 pixels (72k, 2.667 by 1.778 inches) to 2,048 × 3,072 pixels (18Mb, 42.668 by 28.445 inches). In this case, resolution refers to the dimensions of the image in pixels.

A product type of 052/55 denotes Universal Ektachrome, while 116/22 denotes Universal Kodachrome.

2 In the Source Image area, use the Profile pop-up menu to choose a suitable profile. The profile you choose needs to match, if possible, the attributes of the Original Type indicated in the Image Info area. In this example the choice is Universal Ektachrome. If the Medium of the Original is Color Reversal, but you don't know the film type, you can use Universal Kodachrome (Universal-E).

3 In the Destination Image area, specify the resolution at which you want to open the image. The pixel size of the image and the Resolution settings will determine the physical print size of the image when it opens in Photoshop.

4 Select a Color Space. Typically this will be RGB 8 Bits/Channel. OK the Photo CD Plug-in dialog box. The image will open in Photoshop.

Opening an EPS File

EPS files, created in applications such as Adobe Illustrator and Macromedia FreeHand, usually contain object-oriented or "vector" format information. When you open an EPS file in Photoshop, it is rasterized: that is, the vector information is converted into Photoshop's pixel-based format.

1 To open an EPS file as a new document, choose File>Open. Locate and highlight an EPS picture to be opened, then click the Open button. Alternatively, double-click the file name.

2 In the Rasterize dialog box, choose a unit of measurement from the pop-up menus next to the Height and Width fields, and enter new dimensions if required. Enter the resolution required for your final output device and choose an image mode from the Mode pop-up menu.

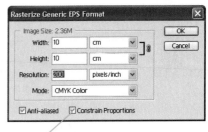

3 Select the Constrain Proportions box to keep the original proportions of the EPS. Select Anti-aliased to slightly blur pixels along edges to avoid unwanted jagged edges. Click OK. The EPS appears in its own image window. It is now a bitmap image.

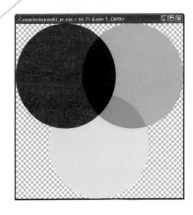

Placing an EPS File

You can also "place" an Illustrator or FreeHand EPS file into an open Photoshop document. Placed EPS files are automatically placed on a new layer.

1   To place an EPS file into an existing Photoshop file, first open an image in Photoshop, or create a new document.

2   Choose File>Place. Use the Place Document dialog box to specify the location and name of the EPS file, then click Place.

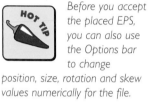

Before you accept the placed EPS, you can also use the Options bar to change position, size, rotation and skew values numerically for the file.

3   A bounding box with eight "handles" and a cross through the placed image will appear in the Photoshop image window. The EPS image itself may take a few seconds to draw inside the bounding box.

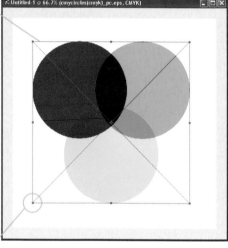

To create anti-aliased edges for a placed EPS, you must select the Anti-aliased option in the Options bar before you click the Accept button.

4   If necessary, drag a corner handle to resize the placed image. Hold down Shift as you drag to maintain proportions. Position your cursor inside the bounding box of the placed image and drag to reposition the image.

If you don't want to accept the placed image, with the bounding box still visible press the Esc key. If you have already placed the image you will have to delete the new layer. (See page 116.)

5   When you are satisfied, press Return/Enter, double-click inside the bounding box, or click the Commit button in the Options bar. The rasterized file is placed on a new layer.

The File Browser

Use the File Browser window to view, manage, sort and open images on your hard disk. You can also use the File Browser to create new folders and to rename, move and delete image files.

1   To show the File Browser window, choose either File>Browser, or Window>File Browser. Use the Folder palette area to navigate to specific folders on your hard disk using standard Macintosh/Windows techniques. You can also use the Folders drop down list, to navigate quickly to recently used folders.

2   Choose an option from the Sort menu to control the way image thumbnails are ordered in the Preview pane. Choose an option from the View menu to control the appearance of thumbnails.

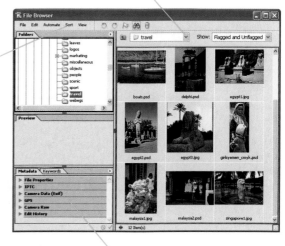

To move a file, position your cursor on the image thumbnail, then drag it to a different folder in the Folder pane of the File Browser window. To copy a file to a new location, hold down Alt/option, then drag it to a different folder.

3   File information for a selected image file appears in the Metadata and Keyword palettes. With the Metadata tab selected, click the expand triangle to the left of Camera Data (Exif) to view image information imported from a digital camera.

4   To open a file from the File Browser, click on a file icon to select it, then press the Enter/Return key. You can also double-click a selected file.

To rank image thumbnails in the Preview pane, choose View>Show Rank, click in the Rank entry box that appears below the image thumbnail, then enter a number. Press Enter/Return. Remember to choose Rank from the Sort menu to order the image thumbnails according to the rank values you enter.

Click the Toggle File Browser button in the Options bar to quickly hide/show the File Browser window:

5 To delete a file, click on the file thumbnail to select it, then either click the Wastebasket icon in the Toolbar, or drag the file onto the Wastebasket. Alternatively, you can press the Delete key.

6 To flag an image, click once on the image thumbnail to select it, then click the Flag file button in the Toolbar at the top of File Browser window. To remove a flag on a thumbnail, first select it, then click the flag button.

egypt2.psd

7 Use the Show drop down menu to restrict the display of image thumbnails in the Preview pane to flagged or unflagged images only. Flagged and Unflagged is the default view.

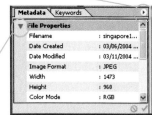

8 Click the Metadata or Keywords tab to view additional labeling information saved with an image. You can also use options from the palette menu for each tab to add and edit metadata and keyword information for your image files.

9 Use the Expand/Collapse triangle to display/hide information for each category.

Saving Files

The basic principles of saving files in Photoshop – using "Save" and "Save As" – are the same as in any other Macintosh or Windows application. Save regularly as you make changes to an image so you do not lose changes you have made should a system crash occur. You should use Save As to save a new file in the first instance, to make copies of a file, to save a file to a new location and when you need to save an image in a different file format.

Photoshop supports numerous file formats for opening and saving images. Typically, you save an image in a particular format to meet specific output or printing specifications, to compress the image to save disk space, or to open or import the image into an application that requires a particular file format.

I   To save an image in the first instance, choose File>Save As. Specify where you want to save the file. Enter a name for the file. Use the Format pop-up to choose an appropriate format. Click the Save button. File extensions are added automatically.

2   To save changes as you work on an image, choose File>Save. The previously saved file information is updated.

Photoshop format

Use this format as you work on your image. Applications such as QuarkXPress will not import images in Photoshop format, but all of Photoshop's options, in particular layers, remain available to you in this format. Photoshop also performs open and save routines more quickly when using its native format.

TIFF Format

TIFF (Tagged Image File Format), originally developed by Aldus, became a standard file format for scanned images in the early days of desktop publishing. It is common on both Mac and Windows platforms and is usable in most paint, image-editing and page layout applications.

On the Macintosh, choose Photoshop> Preferences> File Handling to specify whether or not you want file extensions – e.g. ".tif" – automatically added when saving files.

1 To save an image in TIFF format, choose File>Save As. The Save As dialog box appears. Specify where you want to save the image and enter a name in the name entry box. Use the Format pop-up menu to choose TIFF, then click OK.

2 The TIFF Options dialog box will appear. Select Byte Order options and LZW Compression as required, then OK the dialog box.

Byte Order

Some applications cannot open or import files saved with JPEG or Zip compression.

Use this option to specify whether you want the TIFF to be used on a Mac or a PC, as Mac and PC TIFF formats vary slightly. Most recently released applications can read files using either option.

LZW Compression

A warning appears at the bottom of the Save As dialog box if an image uses features, such as layers or alpha channels, that are not supported by that particular file format. You are prompted to save a copy of the file. Photoshop automatically adds the word "copy" to the file name.

(Lempel-Zif-Welch) is a compression format that looks for repeated elements in the computer code that describes the image and replaces these with shorter sequences. It is a "lossless" compression scheme – none of the image's detail is lost. Applications such as QuarkXPress, Adobe PageMaker, Adobe InDesign and Macromedia FreeHand can import TIFFs with LZW compression.

⚠ **File must be saved as a copy with this selection.**

Zip

Zip is a lossless compression format and achieves greatest compression in images that contain areas of solid color. Zip compression is supported by PDF and TIFF file formats.

JPEG

JPEG is a "lossy" compression format (see page 47). JPEG compression is most suitable for photographic type images with variations in highlight and shadow detail throughout the image. (See page 197 for further information on choosing quality options for JPEG compression.)

Save Image Pyramid

Although Photoshop itself cannot work with multiple resolutions in the same file, you can select the Save Image Pyramid option to preserve multiple resolutions already in a file. Some applications (such as Adobe InDesign) provide support for opening multiresolution files.

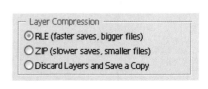

Save Transparency

For images that contain transparent areas you can select Save Transparency. Transparent areas are saved in an additional Alpha channel when the file is opened in a different application. Transparency is always retained when a file is opened in Photoshop.

Layer Compression

Photoshop can read layer information saved in TIFF file format, although most other applications cannot. Files saved with layers are larger than image files that have been flattened into a single layer. Choose Layer Compression options to specify how pixel data in layers is compressed. RLE (Run Length Encoding) is a lossless compression format supported by many Windows file formats. Select Discard Layers and Save a Copy if you do not want to preserve layers in the image.

Photoshop EPS

EPS is generally more reliable for PostScript printing than the TIFF file format, but generates file sizes which can be three to four times greater than TIFFs with LZW compression. To save in EPS format, do the following:

> Follow the procedure for saving TIFFs, but choose Photoshop EPS from the Format pop-up menu. Click OK. The EPS Options dialog box will appear. Specify your settings, then click OK.

Preview

This option specifies the quality of the low-resolution screen preview you see when you import the image into applications such as Adobe InDesign and QuarkXPress. Use "Macintosh (8bits/pixel)" for a color preview. "Macintosh (JPEG)" uses JPEG compression routines, but is only supported by PostScript Level 2 printers. Use TIFF if you want to use the image in Windows.

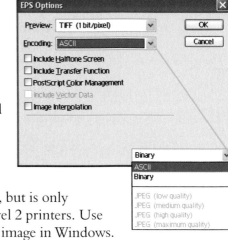

Encoding

Use binary encoding if you want to export the image for use with Adobe Illustrator. Some applications do not recognize binary encoding; in this case you have to use ASCII.

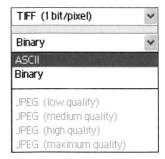

JPEG Format

JPEG is an acronym for Joint Photographic Experts Group. It is an extremely efficient compression format and is frequently used for images on the World Wide Web. JPEG format is available when saving grayscale, RGB and CMYK images.

The JPEG compression routine is a "lossy" procedure. To make the file size of the image smaller, image data is discarded, resulting in reduced image quality.

1 Follow the procedure for saving in TIFF format, but choose JPEG from the Format pop-up menu. OK the Save As dialog box.

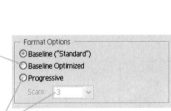

2 Use the Quality pop-up to specify the amount of compression, or drag the slider. Maximum gives best image quality, retaining most of the detail in an image, but results in the least compression. Low gives lowest image quality, but gives maximum compression.

Older browsers cannot display baseline-optimized images.

JPEG is a cumulative compression scheme – if you close an image, then reopen it and then resave it in JPEG format, you will apply a further compression to the image, effectively losing more color information from the image. Save to JPEG format only after you finish all work on an image.

3 In the Format Options area, select Baseline Optimized to optimize the color quality of the image.

4 Select Progressive and enter a value for Scans if you'll use the image on the World Wide Web and want the image to download in a series of passes adding detail progressively.

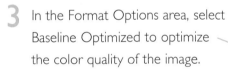

5 The compressed file size is indicated in the Size area. Choose a modem speed from the Size pop-up to see an estimated download time for the image at the specified modem speed.

Creating a New File

Whilst the New dialog box is active, if you have an image already open, you can choose Window, then click the name of any open image file listed at the bottom of the menu; the New dialog box will update with the settings from the file you selected.

When you need a fresh, completely blank canvas to work on, you can create a new file.

1. To create a new file, choose File>New. Enter a name for the new document (or leave this as Untitled and do a Save As later).

Photoshop creates a new file with square pixels by default. Click the Advanced expand button ( ), then use the Pixel Aspect Ratio drop down menu to choose an aspect ratio other than square:

2. Specify Width and Height settings, or choose dimensions from the Preset menu. If you have copied pixels to the clipboard, the

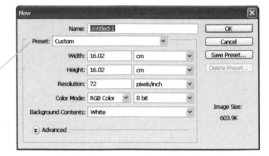

Preset menu is automatically set to Clipboard and the Width and Height fields automatically reflect the dimensions of the elements on the clipboard.

3. Enter a resolution and choose a color mode. You can also specify whether you want to create a file with 8-bits per channel, or 16-bits per channel.

To specify a different Pixel Aspect Ratio for an existing image, choose Image>Pixel Aspect Ratio. Select an aspect ratio from the sub-menu.

4. Select one of the Background Contents options to specify the canvas background you want to begin with, then OK the dialog box.

You can also use the Fill command to fill selections with color.

5. To change the color of the canvas after you have clicked OK in the New dialog box, select a foreground color (see Chapter Five, "Defining Colors"). Next, choose Edit>Fill. Choose Foreground Color from the Use pop-up.

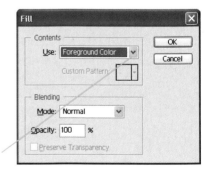

Make sure Opacity is set to 100% and Mode is Normal. Click OK.

Photomerge

The Photomerge command allows you to combine two or more images to create a panorama.

1 Open the images you want to use for the photomerge composition. Choose File>Automate>Photomerge.

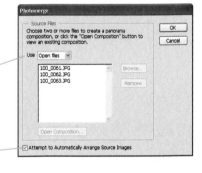

2 In the Photomerge dialog box make sure the Use drop down menu is set to Open Files – these are the files already open in Photoshop. Leave the Attempt to Automatically Arrange Source Images option selected to allow Photoshop to attempt to match and blend the source images automatically. Deselect this option if you want to arrange the individual source images yourself. If Photoshop is unable to arrange the images automatically a warning dialog box appears. OK the warning and arrange the images manually.

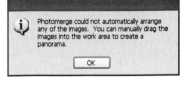

You can drag source image thumbnails out of the lightbox area to become part of the photomerge composition and you can also drag images out of the work area back into the lightbox to remove them from the photomerge composition.

3 To manually create the photomerge composition, drag the source image thumbnails that appear in the lightbox area at the top of the Photomerge window into the main composition work area. Use the Select Image tool ( ) to reposition the images.

The lightbox area allows you to store source images not currently in use in the photomerge composition.

4 If necessary, with the Select Image tool selected, position your cursor on an image in the work area, then drag to reposition each image manually. Use the Rotate Image ( ) tool to rotate images in the work area.

5 Make sure you leave the Snap to Image option selected to allow Photoshop to analyze the images and automatically locate and position areas of common pixel values. Select the Keep as Layers option to save the individual source images on separate layers. This can be useful if you need to color correct individual source images at a later stage.

Use standard Photoshop techniques to zoom in and out on the image and to move around in the work area. You can also use the Navigator view box in the same way as you use the Navigator palette in the Photoshop window:

6 To reduce the effect of color differences in the original source images select the Advanced Blending option. This option blends variations in color and tones in areas of detail over small restricted areas, whilst broad colors and tones are blended over larger areas.

7 To open the photomerge composition in the main Photoshop window click the OK button. To save the composition without opening it in Photoshop click the Save Composition as button.

Getting Started with Images

There are a number of common techniques and tasks, such as cropping an image and making it larger or smaller, or changing the resolution to suit your final output needs, that you need to undertake on many of the images on which you work. This chapter covers a range of these tasks.

Covers

Chapter Four

Rotating an Image

You can quickly rotate an image if you have scanned it at the wrong orientation, or, for example, if you have imported an image in landscape orientation from a digital camera.

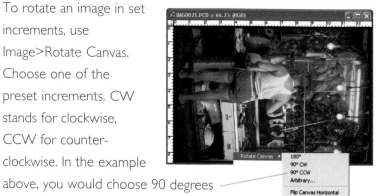

1 To rotate an image in set increments, use Image>Rotate Canvas. Choose one of the preset increments. CW stands for clockwise, CCW for counter-clockwise. In the example above, you would choose 90 degrees counter-clockwise to rotate the Beijing Duck seller upright.

When using arbitrary rotation, position a ruler guide (see page 23, "Ruler Guides and Grids") to help determine how far you need to rotate:

Sometimes you need to adjust an image a few degrees to make up for a poor original photograph or slightly misaligned scan:

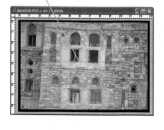

2 To rotate in precise amounts, choose Image>Rotate Canvas>Arbitrary. Enter a value for the angle. Choose the clockwise (CW) or counter-clockwise (CCW) radio button, then OK the dialog box.

3 You may need to recrop the image. Use Unsharp mask to compensate for any blurring due to the rotation.

Choose Image>Rotate Canvas>Flip Canvas Horizontal/ Vertical to flip the entire image across its vertical/horizontal axis.

Resizing without Resampling

When you make the image smaller without resampling, the pixels get smaller. Effectively, you are increasing the resolution of the image. When you make an image bigger without resampling, the pixels get larger and this can lead to jagged, blocky results. Effectively, you are reducing the resolution of the image.

When you resize an image without resampling, you make the image larger or smaller without changing the total number of pixels in the image. The overall dimensions of the image change, the file size remains the same, but the resolution of the image goes up if you make the image smaller, down if you make the image larger.

Smaller without resampling

Original

Larger without resampling

1 To decrease the size of your image without resampling, choose Image>Image Size. Make sure that Resample Image is deselected. Enter a lower value in the Width or Height entry boxes, or enter a higher resolution. The other measurements update automatically. The file size of the image remains the same – no pixels have been added. The resolution has increased – the same number of pixels are packed into a smaller area.

2 To increase the size of your image without resampling, enter a higher value in the Width or Height entry box, or enter a lower resolution. The file size of the image remains the same, but the resolution has decreased.

Resampling Up

Resampling up involves interpolation. Interpolation is used when Photoshop has to add information – new pixels – that didn't previously exist to an image. Choose an interpolation option from the pop-up in the Image size dialog box. Bicubic gives best results, but takes longest. Nearest Neighbor is quickest, but least accurate. Bilinear gives a medium quality result. Bicubic Smoother is intended for enlarging images; Bicubic Sharper for reducing the size of images.

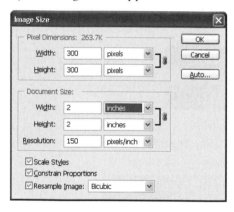

When you resample up, new pixels are added to the image, so the file size increases. Resampling takes place when you increase the resolution setting, or the width/height settings with the Resample Image option selected.

This example starts with a 2in by 2in image at 150 ppi.

As far as possible, try to avoid resampling up. You are adding pixels to the image, without increasing the quality and detail in the image. You get better results if you scan the image at the size at which you intend to use it and at the resolution required for output.

1 Choose Image>Image Size. To keep the overall dimensions of the image, but increase the resolution, make sure that Resample Image is selected. Select Constrain Proportions so that the image's original proportions are maintained. Enter a higher value in the Resolution box.

To reset the dialog box to its original settings, hold down Alt/option on the keyboard. The Cancel button becomes a Reset button. Click the Reset button.

2 The file size and total number of pixels increase, but the Width and Height settings remain the same.

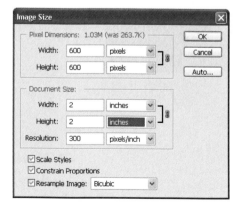

You now have an image which is the same overall size, but which has more pixels in the same area, and therefore its resolution is increased:

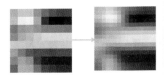

3 To make the overall dimensions of the image bigger, but to keep the same resolution, again make sure that Resample Image is selected. Select Constrain Proportions to keep width and height proportional. Enter a higher value in either the Width or Height entry boxes. (The other entry boxes will update automatically if you have selected Constrain Proportions.)

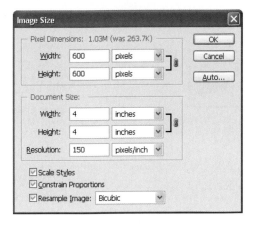

4 The overall dimensions of the image have now increased. The file size and total number of pixels have also increased, but the resolution remains the same.

Sampling Down

You sometimes need to resample down to maintain an optimal balance between the resolution needed for acceptable final output and file size considerations. There is little point in working with an image at too high a resolution if some of the image information is redundant at final output.

Resampling down means discarding pixels. The result is a smaller file size. Resampling down occurs when you decrease the resolution setting, or the width/ height settings with the Resample Image option selected.

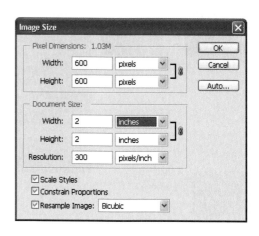

These examples start with a 2 by 2 inch image at 300 ppi.

Choose View>Print Size to get a representation on screen of the physical size of the image when printed.

Choose Image>Image Size. To keep the overall dimensions of the image, but decrease the resolution, make sure that Resample Image is selected. Leave Constrain Proportions selected, so that the image's original proportions are maintained. Reduce the value in the Resolution box.

2 The file size goes down and the total number of pixels decreases, whilst the Width and Height settings remain the same.

You now have an image which is the same overall size, but with fewer pixels in the same area, and therefore its resolution is decreased:

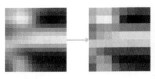

3 To reduce the overall dimensions of the image, but keep the image at the same resolution, make sure that Resample Image is selected. (Select Constrain Proportions to keep the width and height proportional.)
Enter a lower value in either the Width or Height entry box. (The other entry box updates automatically if you select Constrain Proportions.)

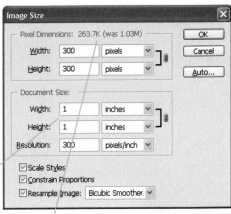

4 The overall dimensions of the image have now decreased. The file size and the total number of pixels have also decreased, but the resolution remains the same.

Cropping an Image

Use the Crop tool to crop unwanted areas of an image and reduce the file size.

Press C on the keyboard to select the Crop tool, then press Return/Enter to show the Crop tool Options bar if it is not already showing.

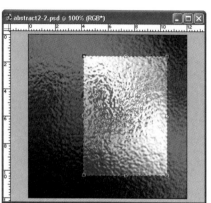

1 Select the Crop tool. Position your cursor on the image, then click and drag to define the crop area. Don't worry if you don't get the crop exactly right first time. The area of the image outside the crop dims to indicate the parts of the image that will be discarded.

With a crop marquee active, use the Shield Cropped Area option in the Options bar to hide/show the crop shading overlay. You can also change the color and/or opacity of the crop shading:

2 To reposition the crop marquee, place your cursor inside the marquee, then click and drag. To resize the crop marquee, place your cursor on one of the 8 handles around the marquee (the cursor changes to a bi-directional arrow), then click and drag. To rotate the marquee, position your cursor just outside the marquee (the cursor changes shape to indicate rotation), then click and drag in a circular direction.

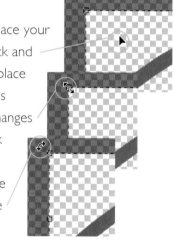

Hold down Shift, then click and drag on a corner handle to resize the crop marquee in proportion.

The Crop tool snaps to the edge of the image. To prevent the snap effect, hold down Command/Ctrl as you resize the crop marquee.

3 When you are satisfied with the position and size of the crop marquee, click the Commit button in the Options bar, or press Return/Enter to crop the image. Alternatively, you can double-click inside the crop marquee. The areas outside the marquee are discarded. Click the Cancel button, or press the Esc key if you want to remove the crop marquee without cropping.

Adding a Border

Borders are useful when you need additional space around the edges of your image.

1. Choose Image>Canvas Size. Use the measurement pop-up menus to choose a unit of measurement. Enter increased values for the Width and/or Height fields.

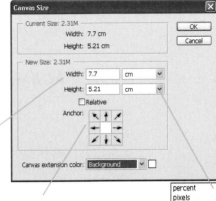

2. To specify where the border is added relative to the image, click one of the placement squares. This sets the relative position of the image and the border. The white square represents the position of the image, the other squares the position of the border.

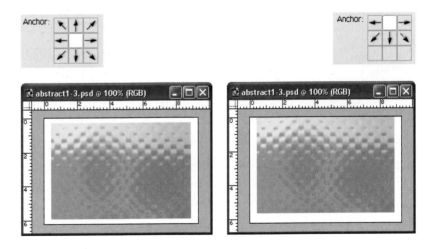

3. Choose a color from the Canvas extension color pop-up menu to specify the color of the border. OK the dialog to add the border.

Image Modes

Image modes are fundamental to working in Photoshop. When you open an image the mode is indicated in the title bar of the image window. There are eight different modes in Photoshop. Use modes as appropriate to your working requirements. Then, depending on output or printing requirements, if necessary, convert to a different mode.

RGB mode

Images are typically scanned or captured in RGB mode. When you start work with a color image it is usually best to work in RGB mode, as this is faster than CMYK mode and allows you to use all of Photoshop's commands and features, providing greatest flexibility.

The disadvantage of working in RGB mode, if your image will be printed, is that RGB allows a greater gamut of colors than you can print. At some stage, some of the brightest, most vibrant colors may lose their brilliance when the image is brought within the CMYK gamut.

CMYK mode

Convert to CMYK when the image is to be printed and you have finished making changes.

You can retain the flexibility of working in RGB mode, but see an on-screen CMYK preview of your image, by choosing View>Proof Colors. (You may have to wait a few seconds when you choose this option as Photoshop builds its color conversion tables.) The title bar of the image changes to indicate that you are working with an RGB image, but previewing in CMYK:

`chillies2.psd @ 50% (RGB/8/CMYK)`

To place a color image in a page layout application from where it will be color separated, you need to convert from RGB to CMYK. When you convert from RGB to CMYK, Photoshop adjusts any colors in the RGB image that fall outside the CMYK gamut to their nearest printable color. (See Chapter Five, "Defining Colors", for details on gamut warnings.)

You can also select View>Gamut Warning (Command/Ctrl+Shift+Y), to highlight (in gray) areas of the image that are out of gamut.

Indexed Color mode

This mode reduces your image to 256 colors or less and is frequently used for multimedia and Web images.

Duotone

For details on using Duotone mode see page 62.

You must first convert to Grayscale mode before you can convert to Duotone mode.

Grayscale mode

When you are not printing an image in color you can convert to Grayscale mode to make working faster and file size smaller.

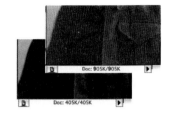

Lab mode

This mode uses the CIE Lab model which has one channel for luminosity, an "a" channel representing colors blue to yellow and a "b" channel for magenta to green. A significant advantage to this mode is that its gamut encompasses that of both CMYK and RGB modes.

Bitmap mode

This mode reduces everything to black or white pixels. The image becomes a 1-bit image.

Multichannel mode

Multichannel mode uses 256 levels of gray in each channel. When you convert RGB or CMYK images to multichannel mode, the original channels in the image are converted to spot color channels. Multichannel mode is an advanced option – only use it if you have a detailed understanding of the printing process.

To convert from one mode to another, choose Image>Mode and choose the mode you want from the sub-menu. Depending on which mode you are converting from and to, you may get a message box warning you of any consequences of converting to the new mode and asking you to confirm your request.

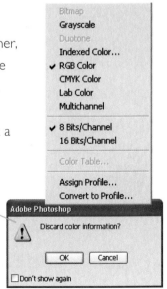

Duotone Mode

You can only access Duotone mode when you have converted to Grayscale mode.

Duotone is a very popular effect used to give added tonal depth to a grayscale image by printing with black and another color.

To create a duotone, choose Image>Mode>Duotone. Choose from the Type pop-up whether you want to create a duotone (two inks), a tritone (three inks) or a quadtone (four inks).

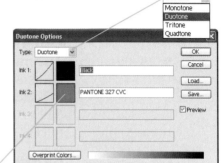

When you start working with Photoshop, click on the Load button and try using one of the preset duotone settings that can be found in: Program Files>ADOBE> Photoshop CS>Presets> Duotones.

To choose a second color for the duotone, click the "Ink 2" color box (below the black ink box). This takes you into the Custom Colors dialog box. Choose a color. Click the Picker button if you want to use the Color Picker. OK the dialog box.

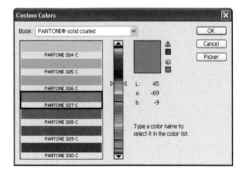

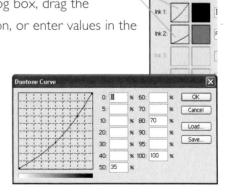

To specify the ink coverage for both colors, click first on the Ink 1 Curve box, then the Ink 2 box. In the Duotone Curve dialog box, drag the curve to the desired position, or enter values in the % entry boxes to adjust the ink coverage curve. Click Preview in the Duotone Options dialog to preview the result in the image window before you OK the dialog boxes.

Make sure you save duotones in EPS format so that they color-separate correctly from page layout applications.

Defining Colors

Defining colors is an essential aspect of using Photoshop and there is a range of techniques that can be used. The color controls in the Toolbox indicate the current foreground and background colors.

Covers

Chapter Five

Foreground & Background Colors

The foreground color is applied when you first create type, and when you use the Paint Bucket, Line, Pencil, and Brush tools.

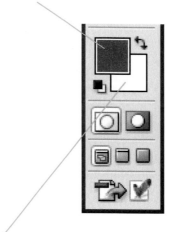

The background color is the color you erase to when you use the Eraser tool, or when you delete or move a selection.

When you are working with foreground and background controls you can also switch colors, and you can quickly change back to the default colors, black and white.

You can change the background and foreground colors using the Eyedropper tool, the Color Picker palette, the Color palette and the Swatches palette.

| To switch background to foreground and vice versa, click once on the Switch Colors arrow.

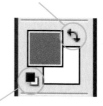

2 To revert to black and white as the default background and foreground colors, click the Default Colors icon.

Eyedropper & Color Sampler Tools (I)

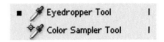

The Eyedropper tool

The Eyedropper tool provides a quick and convenient way to pick up foreground and background color from an area of the image you are working on, or from another inactive Photoshop image window.

1 To set the foreground color, click on the Eyedropper tool. Position your cursor, then click once on the image. The Set foreground color box in the Toolbox now represents the color where you clicked.

2 To set the background color, hold down Alt/option then click on the image. The Set background color box in the Toolbox now indicates the color on which you clicked.

3 To set the Sample Size, use the Sample Size pop-up menu in the Options bar to choose a value. Point Sample reads the precise value of the pixel on which you click. 3 by 3 and 5 by 5 take average values of the pixels where you click.

in the bar

The Color Sampler tool

Shows w/ Eyedroper tool, and stay w/color Sampler

Use the Color Sampler tool (with the Info palette) to set up to four sample points which you can refer to as you make adjustments to color values. Each time you click in the image window with the Color Sampler tool, you set a sample point. Each point creates an extra pane in the Info palette. To delete a sample point, drag it out of the image window with the Color Sampler tool.

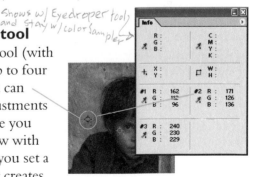

To hide/show the sample points, choose Hide/ Show Color Samplers from the Info palette menu.

The Color Picker Palette

A powerful and flexible way of choosing foreground and background colors is using the Color Picker palette. You can use a number of different color models to create color.

Press the Tab key to move the highlight through the entry boxes in the dialog box.

A warning triangle – the Gamut alarm – will appear next to the Current/ Previous color boxes if you create a color that cannot be printed using CMYK inks. Click the warning triangle to choose the nearest printable color.

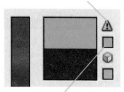

The small box below the warning triangle indicates the nearest printable color.

1 To create a Process color using the Color Picker, click once on either the Set foreground or Set background color box.

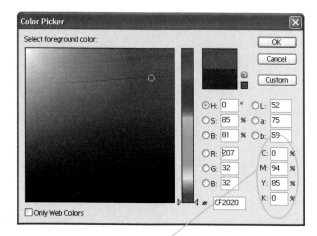

2 Enter values in the CMYK entry boxes. You will see a preview of the color in the Current Color swatch, above the Previous Color swatch.

3 OK the dialog box. The color you defined now becomes the foreground or background color, depending on which box you clicked in Step 1.

You can also create colors using the Color Slider and the Color field. The next example uses Hue, Saturation and Brightness values. Use the same techniques for Red, Green, Blue (RGB) and Lab color models.

To create a color using Hue, Saturation and Brightness (HSB) values, first click the Hue (H) radio button.

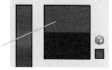

2 Click on the Color Slider bar, or drag the slider triangles on either side of the bar, to choose a hue or color. This sets one of the three HSB values. The number in the Hue entry box represents the hue you have chosen (0–360).

3 Next, click in the Color Field to set the other two variables – Saturation and Brightness. Clicking to the left of the field reduces the saturation, clicking to the right increases the saturation of the selected hue. Clicking near the bottom decreases brightness, clicking near the top increases brightness for the selected hue.

4 If you click on the Saturation button, the Color Slider now represents saturation (from 0–100) and the Color field allows you to choose Hue and Brightness values. When you click the Brightness radio button, the slider represents Brightness and the Color field represents Hue and Saturation.

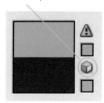

If the Web Colors Only option is deselected, the Non-Web Color alert appears if you create a color that is not in the Web palette. Click the Web alert icon to move the color to the nearest Web-safe color.

Web-safe colors

To create a Web-safe color, select the Only Web Colors option. Fewer colors are represented in the Color Field; each color exists in the Web palette which consists of 216 colors.

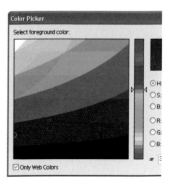

Selecting **PANTONE** Colors

You can access a range of color-matching systems using the Color Picker dialog box. These include: Toyo Color Finder 1050 System, Focoltone Color System, PANTONE Matching System, Trumatch Swatching System and DIC Color Guide. Here, we'll select a PANTONE color.

To select a PANTONE color, click the Set foreground or Set background color box. The Color Picker dialog box will appear. Click the Custom button.

Use the Book pop-up menu to select a PANTONE matching system.

In the Custom Colors dialog box, click the Picker button to return to the Color Picker dialog box.

If you know the PANTONE number of the color you want, you can enter the number on the

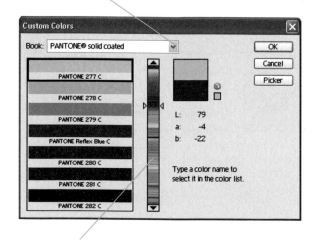

keyboard. Alternatively, click in the color slider bar to the right of the PANTONE color boxes. This moves you to a general range of colors. Then click on the scroll bars at the top and bottom of the sliders to find the specific PANTONE color you want.

Click on the color you want to select, then click OK.

The Color Palette

You can also use the Color palette (Window> Colors) to mix new colors.

1 First identify which color selection box is "active". There are two boxes, Set foreground color and Set background color. The active box is outlined in black.

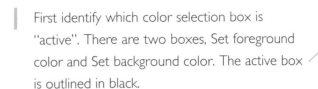

2 Continue with step 3 if the correct box is active, or click the inactive box to make it the active box if necessary.

3 Drag the Color slider triangles below the Color slider bars, or enter values in the entry boxes to the right of the palette. You can also click on a color in the Color Bar running along the bottom of the Color palette. The Color Bar contains every color in the CMYK spectrum as a default setting.

4 Use the palette menu triangle in the top right of the palette to change the color model for the sliders.

5 Choose an option from the bottom half of the palette menu to specify the color model for the colors in the Color Bar at the bottom of the palette.

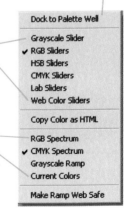

The Swatches Palette

You can use the Swatches palette (Window>Show Swatches) to set foreground and background colors, and you can also use it to create custom palettes which you can save and then reload into a different image.

See page 28 for details on loading and saving custom palette settings.

1 To select a foreground color from the Swatches palette, click on a color swatch. To select a background color, hold down Command/Ctrl and then click on a color swatch.

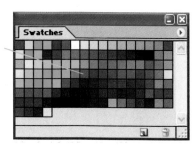

You can customize the Swatches palette by adding and deleting colors in the palette.

2 To add color to the swatches, select a foreground color. Position your cursor in an empty area of the Swatches palette. (The cursor changes to a paint bucket.) Then click. Enter a name for the new swatch, then click OK to add the current foreground color to the Swatches palette.

Position your cursor on a swatch in the Swatches palette, hold down Control (Mac), or click the right mouse button (PC) to access the context sensitive menu:

New Swatch...
Rename Swatch...
Delete Swatch

3 To delete a color swatch, hold down Alt/option (Mac) or Alt (Windows) and then click on a color swatch.

4 Use the Swatches palette menu to reset the Swatches palette to its default settings, or to choose a different color palette from the list.

The Painting Tools

The Brush and Pencil tools apply the foreground color to pixels in your image as you drag across them. By default, the Brush tool creates strokes with softened edges and the Pencil tool creates hard-edged lines. You can use the Brushes palette to determine the shape, size and type of brush stroke and to customize the brush shape and brush dynamics – the way the brush behaves as it colors pixels.

You can also save a customized brush as a "preset" brush. This allows you to create your own collection of custom brush effects that you can access quickly and easily whenever you need to.

Covers

Chapter Six

The Brush Pop-up Palette

The Brush Pop-up palette allows quick, convenient access to a range of standard, preset brushes.

Rest your cursor on the brush thumbnail in the scroll box to see a descriptive help label for the tool.

When you make changes to Mode, Opacity and Flow in the Options bar, these settings remain in force when you choose a different brush from the Brush Pop-up palette.

For circular shape brushes, use the Hardness slider to increase/decrease the hardness setting for the edge of the brush. (See page 78 for further information on setting Hardness).

To constrain your painting strokes to straight lines, click with the Painting tool to position the start of the stroke, move your cursor (do not click and drag) then hold down Shift and click to end the stroke.

1 To select a brush, click on the Brush tool to select it, then click the Brush pop-up triangle icon in the Options bar.

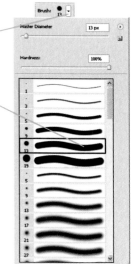

2 Click on a brush you want to use in the scroll box. A representation of the shape of the brush appears in the left column of the scroll box, a thumbnail of the stroke appears to the right. The number beneath the brush icon indicates the diameter of the brush in pixels.

3 To change the size of the brush, drag the Master Diameter slider to increase/decrease the size of the brush, or enter a value in pixels in the Size Entry box. Click the Use Sample Size button to return to the original size of the brush if you have made changes to the Master Diameter. (This option is only available for brush tip shapes created originally from a sample of pixels).

4 Create settings for Mode, Opacity and Flow in the Options bar and choose the Airbrush option if required.

5 Position your cursor in the image window, then press and drag to apply the foreground color using the current brush characteristics and the brush settings in the Options bar.

Remember to choose the foreground color you want to paint with before you start to use a painting tool.

To change the Opacity setting using the keyboard, type numbers on the keyboard. For example, type 7 to specify an Opacity setting of 70%. Type 7 then 8 in quick succession to create a setting of 78%.

For a description of blending modes, see pages 82–84.

Opacity

Opacity (Brush, Pencil, History Brush, Art History Brush, Gradient, Paint Bucket, Clone Stamp and Pattern Stamp tools) controls how completely pixels are covered with the foreground color when you drag across them.

Make sure the Opacity slider is at 100% if you want to completely cover the pixels you drag across. (Soft-edged brushes only partially cover pixels around the edge of the painting stroke to create the soft edge effect.) Reducing the Opacity setting gives less complete results in the area you drag across, creating a semi-transparent, partially-covered effect.

Opacity = 100%

Opacity = 50%

Opacity = 20%

Flow

Flow controls how quickly paint is applied when you drag the brush across the image.

Flow = 100%

Flow = 30%

Airbrush

Select the Airbrush option to imitate the effect of spraying paint with an airbrush. The Airbrush option works best with soft-edged brushes and reduced Opacity and Flow settings.

Flow = 100%

Opacity = 50%

The Brushes Palette

The Brushes palette provides access to a wide variety of options for controlling the appearance and characteristics of your brush strokes. You can use preset brushes, or you can create your own custom brushes using a variety of interchangeable settings.

If the Brushes palette appears dimmed, you do not have an appropriate Painting or Editing tool selected.

1 To create custom brush characteristics, select a painting tool. By default, the Brushes palette is docked in the Palette Well (on the right-hand side of the Options bar). Click on the Brushes tab to display the Brushes palette.

Drag the Brushes tab from the Palette Well if you prefer the palette to behave as a standard floating palette.

2 Make sure the Brush Presets option is selected. Click on a preset brush in the scroll list. You can rest your cursor on a preset brush in the scroll list to show a help label which indicates the settings currently applied to the brush. Depending on the brush preset you click on, the various customized settings already applied to the brush, visible in the left hand column, change accordingly.

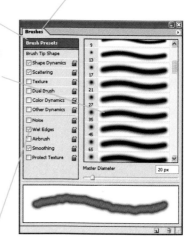

You can also use the Brushes palette for setting the brush characteristics for Editing tools.

3 To customize the preset brush by adding your own brush settings, removing existing settings, click the Check boxes to the left of the brush characteristic labels. The preview pane at the bottom of the palette updates to indicate the effect on the brush. (In this example the 35-pixel, soft-edged brush is selected, with Scattering Wet Edges and Smoothing also applied.)

4 Drag the Master Diameter slider to change the size of the brush, or enter a value in pixels in the Size Entry box.

5 Click on the Brush Tip Shape button to change shape settings such as Angle, Roundness, Hardness and Spacing if required. (See page 78 for further information.)

Selecting the Airbrush option in the Options palette is the equivalent of selecting Airbrush from the effects list in the Brushes palette.

6 Click the brush characteristic label (to the right of the Check box) to access a range of controls for the option.
(See page 76 for information on creating custom brush characteristic settings).

7 Create settings for Mode, Opacity and Flow in the Options bar.

Use the Brush Pop-up palette when you want to quickly select a brush from the existing set of brushes. Use the Brushes palette to select a preset brush and also to create and design your own custom brushes.

8 If you click on a different brush in the scroll list, any custom settings for the previously selected brush are lost.

9 Position your cursor in the image window, then click and drag to create the required paint stroke.

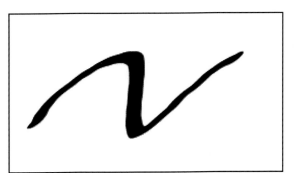

Custom Brush Settings

Preset brushes can be customized using the style options on the left side of the Brushes palette together with the settings which control the Brush Tip Shape. Effects above the gray divider bar have controls that allow you to customize each effect. Style options below the gray divider bar cannot be edited.

1 To create custom settings for a brush effect such as Shape Dynamics, click the effect label (the words Shape Dynamics) – not the Check box. The controls available for each brush effect appear on the right of the dialog box.

To understand what Photoshop refers to as paint marks, select a simple preset brush, click the Brush Tip Shape button, then drag the spacing slider to the right. This indicates visually how the individual paint marks form a paint stroke when you drag the Brush tool in the image window.

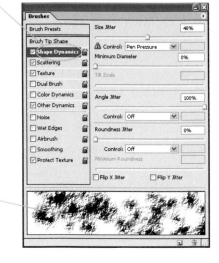

2 Experiment with the settings available. The preview box at the bottom of the palette updates to reflect changes you make to the settings.

Shape Dynamics

The Shape Dynamics options control the manner in which brush marks in the painting stroke change as you drag your cursor in the image window.

Scattering

Scattering settings allow you to specify how the position of the paint marks in a stroke is varied and also control the number of paint marks in a stroke.

Texture

Use texture settings on a brush to associate the brush with a pattern to create paint strokes that appear to be painted on a textured canvas.

Dual Brush

Dual Brush uses two tips to create the brush stroke. Set options for the primary tip using options in the Brush Tip Shape area. Set options for the secondary tip in the Dual Brush area.

Color Dynamics

Color Dynamics settings control how the color of the painting stroke changes over the length of the stroke.

Other Dynamics

Other Dynamics control the speed with which paint is applied and the opacity of the paint in the stroke.

Noise

Noise has the most apparent effect around the edges of soft-edged brushes and creates a random scattering of pixels.

Wet Edges

Wet Edges creates a stroke that is darker around the edges and translucent inside the stroke, imitating the uneven build up of paint in a watercolor.

Airbrush

The Airbrush option on a soft-edged brush with a medium to low Opacity setting simulates the effect of spraying paint with an airbrush.

Smoothing

Smoothing helps create smoother curves in brush strokes.

Protect Texture

Select the Protect Texture option to keep texture effects consistent when painting with different textured brush tips. The option applies the same pattern and scale to all preset brushes with a texture.

Brush Tip Shape Settings

The Brush Tip Shape options area of the Brushes palette provides a further set of controls for specifying the appearance of a brush stroke.

> To create custom brush tip shape settings for a brush, click the Brush Tip Shape button in the Brushes palette. Enter values for Diameter, Hardness, Spacing, Angle and Roundness in the New Brush dialog box.

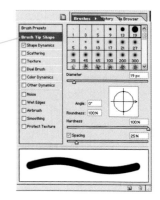

Diameter

Enter a value in pixels for the diameter of your brush from 1–2500. Brush sizes too large to be represented at their actual size will display with the diameter indicated as a number.

Hardness

A setting of 100% gives a hard-edged brush. Settings below 100% produce soft-edged brushes. The lower you take this setting, the more diffuse the resultant stroke when you paint with the brush. Even with a setting of 100%, the edge of the brush-stroke is anti-aliased.

Spacing

Spacing is measured as a percentage of brush size. 25% is the default setting for standard brushes. Higher settings begin to create non-continuous strokes.

To save custom brush tip settings for future use, see page 85 – "Creating Brush Preset Tools".

Angle and Roundness

Use these controls together to create a stroke which thickens and thins like a calligraphic pen. You can enter values in the entry boxes, or drag the arrow indicator to change the angle, and drag the diameter dots to change the diameter.

The Pencil Tool

Pencil Tool   B

You can use the Pencil tool to draw freeform lines. The lines you draw with the Pencil tool are always hard-edged – in other words, the edges of your lines are not anti-aliased. The Pencil tool paints or draws with the foreground color.

1   To draw a line, first select the Pencil tool. Set a brush size using the Brush Pop-up palette. (See page 72). Or use the Brushes palette to create custom brush settings for the tool. (See page 76).

2   Use the Pencil Options bar to specify: Blending Mode, Opacity and Auto Erase options.

Brush: 27   Mode: Normal   Opacity: 100%   ☐ Auto Erase

3   Click and drag to create a freeform pencil stroke. Hold down Shift, then drag to constrain the pencil stroke vertically or horizontally.

4   Click, move the cursor to a new position (do not click and drag), hold down Shift, then click again to create a straight pencil stroke between two points.

Auto Erase
Select this option to use the Pencil tool as an eraser.

The Gradient Tool

Gradient Tool   G

You can use the Gradient tool to create transitions from one color to another. You can also create multicolored gradients. There are options for Linear, Radial, Angle, Reflected and Diamond gradients. You can apply a gradient fill to a selection, or to an entire active layer.

1   To create a gradient fill, select the Gradient tool. Choose a gradient type from the Options bar.

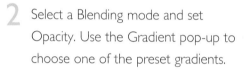

Hold down Shift as you click and drag to constrain a linear gradient to 45-degree increments.

2   Select a Blending mode and set Opacity. Use the Gradient pop-up to choose one of the preset gradients.

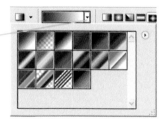

3   Position your cursor where you want the gradient to start, then click and drag. The angle and distance you drag the cursor defines the angle and distance of a linear gradient, or the radius of a radial gradient. (Click and drag from the center out to create Radial, Angle, Reflected and Diamond gradient fills.)

For a linear gradient, the start and end colors fill any part of the selection that you do not drag the cursor across. For radial gradients, the end color fills the remaining area.

4   For basic gradient fills leave the Transparency and Dither options selected. Choose the Reverse option to reverse the order of the colors in the gradient.

Linear

Radial

Angle

Reflected

Diamond

The Paint Bucket Tool

■  Paint Bucket Tool   G

You can use the Paint Bucket tool to color pixels with the foreground color, based on a tolerance setting. It works in a similar way to the Magic Wand tool, but in this case filling adjoining pixels that fall within the tolerance setting. You can use the Paint Bucket tool within a selection or on the entire image.

1 To fill an area with the foreground color, select the Paint Bucket tool. Leave the Fill pop-up set to Foreground. Enter a value from 0–255 in the Tolerance box. The higher you set the value, the greater the pixel range the Paint Bucket will fill.

The Anti-aliased option creates a slightly soft edge on the areas that the Paint Bucket fills.

2 Set Opacity, Blending mode, Anti-aliased and All Layers options as required. Position your cursor then click on the image.

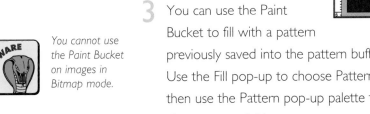

You cannot use the Paint Bucket on images in Bitmap mode.

3 You can use the Paint Bucket to fill with a pattern previously saved into the pattern buffer. Use the Fill pop-up to choose Pattern, then use the Pattern pop-up palette to choose an available pattern.

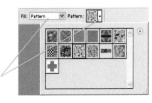

4 Deselect the Contiguous option to allow the Paint Bucket to color pixels anywhere in the image, provided that they fall within the Tolerance setting.

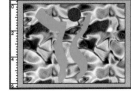

Blending Modes

Normal
Dissolve
Behind
Clear
Darken
Multiply
Color Burn
Linear Burn
Lighten
Screen
Color Dodge
Linear Dodge
Overlay
Soft Light
Hard Light
Vivid Light
Linear Light
Pin Light
Difference
Exclusion
Hue
Saturation
Color
Luminosity

Choose blending modes from the pop-up menu in the Painting Tool Options palette. The various paint modes in combination with opacity/pressure settings have a selective control on which pixels are affected when you use the painting and editing tools. The result is more of a blending of the paint color and the color of the base pixels than simply one color replacing another.

Dissolve

Produces a grainy, chalk-like effect. Not all pixels are colored as you drag across the image, leaving gaps and holes in the stroke. Reduce the Opacity setting to control the effect.

Clear

Makes pixels transparent. You can only access this mode on a layer with the Lock Transparency option deselected. Available for the Brush, Paint Bucket, Pencil and Line tools.

Behind

Only available when you are working on a layer with a transparent background. Make sure Lock Transparency is deselected for the layer. Use Behind to paint behind the existing pixels on a layer. Paint appears in the transparent areas, but does not affect the existing pixels.

 The blending modes allow you to make changes to an image using the painting and editing tools in a more selective and subtle way than simply painting with the foreground color. The color you paint with (the blend color) combines with the color of the pixels you drag across (the base color) to produce a different color depending on the blending mode you select.

Darken

Applies the paint color to pixels that are lighter than the paint color – doesn't change pixels darker than the paint color.

Multiply

Combines the color you are painting with the color of the pixels you drag across, to produce a color that is darker than the original colors.

Color Burn

Darkens the base color by increasing the contrast in base color pixels, depending on the blend color. More pronounced when paint color is dark. Blending with white has no effect.

Linear Burn

Darkens the base color by decreasing brightness depending on the blend color used. Blending with white has no effect.

Lighten

Replaces pixels darker than the paint color, but does not change pixels lighter than the paint color.

Screen

Produces the opposite effect to Multiply. It multiplies the opposite of the original color by the painting color and has the effect of lightening the pixels.

Color Dodge

Brightens the base color by decreasing contrast. More pronounced when the paint color is light. Blending with black has no effect.

Linear Dodge

Brightens the base color by increasing the brightness depending on the blend color. Blending with black has no effect.

Overlay

This increases the contrast and saturation, combining the foreground color with the pixels you drag across. Highlights and shadows in the base color are preserved.

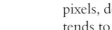
Soft Light

Creates a soft lighting effect. Lightens colors if the painting color is lighter than 50% gray, darkens colors if the painting color is darker than 50% gray.

Hard Light

Multiplies (darkens) or screens (lightens) pixels, depending on the paint color, and tends to increase contrast.

Vivid Light
Burns or Dodges base pixel colors by increasing or decreasing contrast depending on the blend color.

Linear Light
Burns or Dodges base pixel colors by increasing or decreasing brightness depending on the blend color.

Pin Light
Replaces base color pixels depending on whether the blend color is lighter or darker than 50% gray.

Difference
It looks at the brightness of pixels and the paint color, then subtracts paint brightness from pixel brightness. Depending on the result, it inverts the pixels.

Exclusion
The result is similar to Difference, but with lower contrast.

Hue
In color images, applies the hue (color) of the paint, without affecting the saturation or luminosity of the base pixels.

Saturation
Changes the saturation of pixels based on the saturation of the blend color, but does not affect hue or luminosity.

Luminosity
Changes the relative lightness/darkness of the pixels without affecting their hue/saturation.

Color
Applies the hue and saturation of the blend color; does not affect base pixel luminosity.

Creating Brush Preset Tools

Create a Brush tool preset when you have created custom brush settings that you want to be able to reuse, without having to first recreate the custom settings.

1. To create a Brush tool preset, select the Brush tool, then use the Brush palette to create custom settings for the brush.

2. Choose Window> Tool Presets, to show the Tool Presets palette if it is not already showing.

3. Choose New Tool Preset from the palette menu. Enter a name for the tool preset in the New Tool Preset dialog box.

4. To access the new tool preset, make sure you have the Brush tool selected, then click the Brush tool presets triangle in the Options bar. Click on the tool preset in the drop-down list.

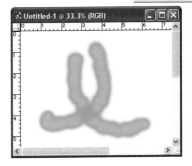

A tool preset allows you to save custom brush settings so that you can access them quickly and easily, whenever you need to, without having to first recreate the settings.

Creating Rasterized Shapes

A rasterized shape is a shape comprised of pixels. It is not based on a vector path and cannot be edited in the same way as a shape layer.

1 To create a rasterized shape, select a layer, or create a new layer. Select a foreground color for the shape.

2 Select either the Rectangle, Rounded Rectangle, Ellipse, Line, Polygon or Custom Shape tool.

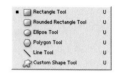

3 Select the Fill Pixels button in the Options bar.

You cannot create a rasterized shape on a vector based shape layer or a type layer.

4 Position your cursor in the image window. Drag diagonally to define the size of the shape. The shape appears in the window.

It does not automatically create a new layer. A rasterized shape is the equivalent of creating a selection, then filling it with a color.

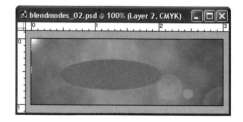

5 For the Polygon tool, you can set a number of sides for the shape in the Options bar. Click on the settings pop-up triangle to access further controls for creating polygons or stars.

The Polygon tool and the Custom Shape tools are not available in ImageReady.

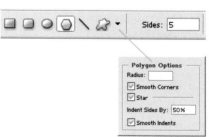

The Editing Tools

The editing tools – Blur and Sharpen, Smudge, Clone and Pattern Stamp, Dodge, Burn, Sponge, Eraser, Healing Brush, Patch and Color Replacement – let you edit or change pixels in a variety of ways.

The editing tools can be used within a selection or anywhere on an image. Use the Brush Pop-up palette to specify a brush size for the editing tool. Many of the techniques and keyboard shortcuts covered for the painting tools apply to the editing tools as well.

Covers

Chapter Seven

The Blur, Sharpen & Smudge Tools

Remember to set an appropriate brush size before you start working with the Blur/Sharpen tool.

The Blur Tool

The Blur and Sharpen tools are the two "focus" tools. The Blur tool works by reducing contrast between pixels and can be useful for disguising unwanted, jagged edges and softening edges between shapes.

> To blur areas of your image, select the Blur tool. If the Blur Options bar is not showing, you can double-click the Blur tool to show it.

You cannot use the Blur/Sharpen tool on an image in Bitmap or Indexed Color mode.

> Set the Blend mode, Strength and Use All Layers options, position your cursor on the image, then click and drag to blur the pixels. Release the mouse then drag across the pixels again to intensify the effect.

The Sharpen Tool

The Sharpen tool works by increasing the contrast between pixels.

> To sharpen areas of an image, select the Sharpen tool. Use the Options bar to create the settings you want to use.

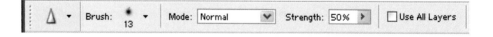

Each Focus tool retains its own settings when you switch to the other tool.

> Position your cursor, then click and drag to sharpen the pixels. Click and drag across the same area of the image again, to intensify the sharpening effect. You will produce a coarse, grainy effect if you overuse the Sharpen tool. Use a low Strength setting and build up the effect gradually.

The Smudge Tool

You can use the Smudge tool to create an effect similar to dragging your finger through wet paint. The Smudge tool picks up color from where you start to drag and smears it into adjacent colors.

Hold down Alt/option to temporarily turn Finger Painting on or off, depending on whether the option is selected in the Options bar.

Select the Smudge tool. Set the Strength, position your cursor on the image, then start to drag across your image to smudge the colors. The higher the Strength setting, the more pronounced the effect.

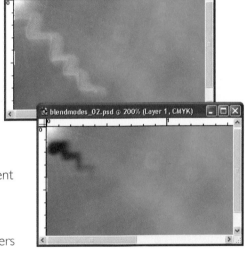

2   Select the Finger Painting option if you want to begin the smudge with the current foreground color.

3   Select the Use All Layers option if you want to smudge colors from other layers in the image onto the layer you are working on. Leave this option deselected if you want the smudge to pick up color from pixels on the active or target layer only.

Use All Layers

Select this option when you want Photoshop to take into account, or "sample", pixels from layers other than the target layer. In other words, it samples from layers as if they were merged.

The Clone Stamp Tool

You can use the Clone Stamp tool to retouch an image by cloning or duplicating areas of it. This is very useful when you want to remove blemishes and scratches.

> To clone an area of your image, select the Clone Stamp tool. Set an appropriate brush size using the Brush Pop-up palette in the Options bar. Make sure that the Aligned option is selected.

Use the "[" or "]" keys on the keyboard to decrease/increase the size of the editing tool brushes as you work.

2 Hold down Alt/option and click on the part of the image you want to clone.

3 Release Alt/option. Move the cursor to a different image part then click and drag. The pixels in the image where you drag are replaced by pixels cloned from the spot where you first clicked. A crosshair at the point where you first clicked indicates the pixels that are being cloned – the source point.

Clone – Aligned
With Aligned selected, the distance from the source point (shown by the crosshair) to the Clone Stamp cursor remains fixed. When you release the mouse, move the cursor, then continue to use the Clone Stamp tool, the relative position of the source point and the Rubber Stamp cursor remains constant, but you will now clone pixels from a different part of the image.

Clone – Non-aligned
With the Aligned option off, the source point – where you first click – remains the same. If you stop dragging with the Clone Stamp cursor, move to a different part of the image, then start dragging again, the pixels you clone continue to come from the original source point.

The Dodge, Burn and Sponge Tools

The Dodge, Burn, Saturate/ Desaturate group of tools are sometimes referred to as the "toning" tools. The Dodge and Burn tools are based on the traditional photographic technique of decreasing the amount of exposure given to a specific area on a print to lighten it (dodging), or increasing the exposure to darken areas (burning-in).

The Dodge Tool
Use the Dodge tool to lighten pixels in your image.

You cannot use the Dodge, Burn or Saturate/ Desaturate tools on an image in Bitmap or Indexed Color mode.

To lighten areas of an image, select the Dodge tool. Remember to choose an appropriate brush size. A soft-edged brush usually creates the smoothest result. If the Options bar is not showing, you can double-click the Dodge tool to show it.

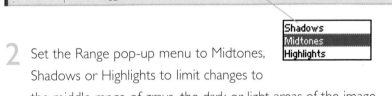

2 Set the Range pop-up menu to Midtones, Shadows or Highlights to limit changes to the middle range of grays, the dark or light areas of the image respectively, and also set Exposure to control the intensity of the tool.

It's a good idea to use a low exposure setting when you lighten areas of an image and build up the effect gradually.

3 Position your cursor on the image, then click and drag to lighten the pixels. Release the mouse then drag across the pixels again to intensify the effect.

The Burn Tool

Use the Burn tool to darken pixels in your image.

1 To darken areas of an image, select the Burn tool. Remember to choose an appropriate brush size. A soft-edged brush usually creates the smoothest result.

2 Set the Range pop-up to Midtones, Shadows or Highlights to limit changes to the middle range of grays, the dark or light areas of the image respectively, and also set Exposure.

3 Position your cursor on the image, then click and drag to darken the pixels. Release the mouse then drag across the pixels again to intensify the effect.

In Grayscale mode, the Sponge tool has the effect of increasing or decreasing contrast.

The Sponge Tool

You can use the Sponge tool when you want to subtly increase or decrease color saturation in areas of your image.

1 To saturate/desaturate areas of an image, select the Sponge tool. Remember to select an appropriate brush size.

Each Toning tool retains its own settings when you switch to the other tools in the same group.

2 Set the Mode pop-up to Saturate or Desaturate and apply a Flow setting.

3 Position your cursor on the image, then click and drag to alter the saturation.

The Eraser Tool

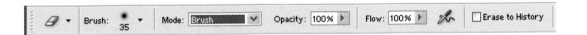

Use the Eraser tool to erase portions of your image. The Eraser rubs out to the background color when you are working on the Background layer. It erases to transparency when you are working on any other layer, provided that the Transparency Lock option is not selected in the Layers palette.

Use the Master Diameter setting in the Brush Pop-up palette to specify the Eraser size when using the tool in Brush and Pencil mode.

To erase areas of your image, select the Eraser tool (E) to show Eraser options in the Options bar. Use the bar to specify brush size, Mode, Opacity, Flow, Airbrush and Erase to History options.

2 Click and drag on your image to erase to the background color or transparency, depending on the layer on which you are working.

Opacity

Use the Opacity setting to create the effect of partially erasing pixels.

Hold down Alt/option with the Eraser tool selected to access the Erase to History option temporarily. Click and drag across modified areas of the image to restore them to the specified state in the History palette.

Mode

Use the Erasing Mode pop-up to choose an erase mode. The default is Brush. Block is useful when you need to erase along straight edges. The Block eraser is a fixed-size square.

Erase to History

Use the Erase to History option to return pixels to their status at a particular state in the History palette. Click in the History Brush column in the History palette to set the state to which the Erase to History option returns pixels.

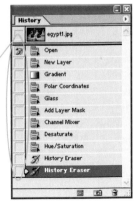

The Magic Eraser

The Magic Eraser tool is grouped with the Eraser tool. Press and hold on the Eraser tool to access the tools in the tool group. You can also use the keyboard shortcut Shift+E to cycle through the Eraser tools.

Use the Magic Eraser tool to erase pixels on a layer to transparency. The Magic Eraser works best when you want to remove the background pixels around a hard-edged object. The Magic Eraser tool erases pixels based on a tolerance level, similar to the way in which the Magic Wand works. (See page 105 for information on the Magic Wand.)

To use the Magic Eraser tool, first select the layer on which you want to work. Select the Magic Eraser tool to show the Magic Eraser options in the Options bar. Enter a Tolerance value. Set a low Tolerance value to erase pixels that are very similar in color value to the pixel on which you first click. Set a high Tolerance value to select a wider range of pixels.

Tolerance: 32   ☑ Anti-aliased   ☑ Contiguous   ☐ Use All Layers   Opacity: 100% ▶

Select the Use All Layers option to erase pixels based on a sample that takes into account color values from all visible layers, not only the currently active layer.

2 Set an Opacity value of 100% to erase pixels completely. Set a lower Opacity value to create a partially transparent effect. Select the Anti-aliased option to create a smoother edge when pixels are erased. (See page 101 for furthe r information on anti-aliasing).

The Tolerance value extends or limits the number of pixels that are erased.

3 Select Contiguous to erase only pixels that fall within the Tolerance value specified, and that are adjacent to each other. This option erases continuous areas of pixels. Deselect Contiguous if you want the Magic Eraser to erase all pixels that fall within the Tolerance value anywhere in the image.

If you use the Magic Eraser on the Background layer, Photoshop automatically converts the layer to Layer 0.

4 Position the cursor, then click to erase pixels that fall within the Tolerance value.

The Background Eraser

Use the Background Eraser tool when you are working on a layer to erase pixels to transparency. You can set tolerance and sampling values to control the level of transparency and the sharpness of its boundary edges.

1 To erase pixels on a layer, select a layer on which you want to work. Select the Background Eraser tool to show its options in the Options bar. Select a brush from the Brush Presets picker.

The Background Eraser tool displays a crosshair at the center of its brush cursor. This indicates the tool's "hotspot" – the point at which the tool's settings have the greatest effect. The settings you choose have the greatest effect at the hotspot. The strength of the effect diminishes further away from the hotspot:

2 Choose Contiguous from the Limits pop-up menu to remove adjacent pixels that fall within the tolerance setting. (Discontiguous erases pixels throughout the image, Find Edges preserves sharp edges along objects).

3 Enter a Tolerance value, or drag the Tolerance slider. Set a low Tolerance value to limit the effect to pixels that are very similar in color value to pixels at the "hotspot". Set a high Tolerance value to erase a broader range of similar colors.

4 Choose a Sampling option. Select Continuous to erase all colors that you drag across. Select Once to erase pixels that are the same color as the pixel on which you first click. This is useful when you want to erase areas of solid color. Select Background Swatch to erase areas containing the current background color.

Select the Protect Foreground Color if you want to prevent the tool from erasing any pixels that match the current foreground color.

5 Position your cursor, then click or drag to erase pixels on the layer to transparency, based on the settings you have chosen.

The Healing Brush Tool

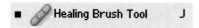 ■ Healing Brush Tool   J

Use the Healing Brush tool to correct flaws and imperfections in an image. The Healing Brush is similar to the Clone Stamp tool in the way it works, but it also matches the texture, luminosity and shading of the sampled pixels to the pixels in the area you want to "heal". This usually produces a more seamless result than the Clone Stamp tool.

To "heal" an imperfection, select the Healing Brush tool. Use the Brush Pop-up palette to choose a brush size. Select a blending mode if required. Use Replace mode to preserve the texture, noise and any film grain at the edges of the brush strokes. Leave the Source option set to Sampled to use pixels from within the image.

2 Select Aligned in the Options bar (see page 90 for information on the Aligned option).

3 Position your cursor on an area of the image that you want to sample from to repair the imperfection. Hold down Alt/option, then click the left mouse button. This sets the sample area of pixels.

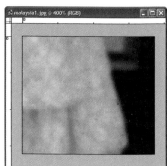

4 Release the Alt/option key. Move your cursor over the area you want to repair. Click, or press and drag to repair the area. When you click or drag the mouse, the (+) indicates the area of the image you are sampling pixels from.

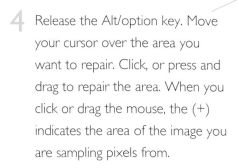

The Patch Tool

The Patch tool allows you to disguise problems and flaws in an image by cloning or copying pixels from another, similar part of the image. The Patch tool attempts to match the texture and shading of the pixels that are copied or sampled to the source pixels – the pixels you are patching over.

You usually achieve the best results with the Patch tool when you select a relatively small area.

1 Select the Patch tool. Select Source in the Options bar. Drag in the image to select the area of pixels you want to patch over.

2 Still working with the Patch tool, position your cursor inside the Patch selection, then drag the selection area onto the area of the image from which you want to copy pixels.

3 Release the mouse button. The original patch selection is repaired with pixels sampled from the area you released on.

4 Alternatively, select Destination in the Options Bar to reverse the way in which the tool works. Use the Patch tool to select the area of pixels you want to use to make the repair. Drag the Patch selection onto the area of pixels you want to repair. Release the mouse to copy the initial selection area over the flaw.

Color Replacement

Use the Color Replacement tool to paint over specific colors in an image. For example, you can use the Color Replacement tool to remove "red eye" in an image.

 See Chapter 5, "Defining Colors" for information on selecting foreground color.

1 To paint over a color, select the Color Replacement tool. Select a foreground color. Create settings such as Diameter using the Brush Pop-up palette in the Options bar. Leave Mode set to Color.

2 For Sampling, choose Continuous to sample and replace colors continuously as you drag. Choose Once to replace only the target color you first click on. This makes the tool very specific and typically changes only a limited number of pixels. Choose Background Swatch to limit color changes to pixels that are the same color as the Background color.

 Leave the Anti-aliased option selected to achieve a smooth edge to the areas where you replace color.

☑ Anti-aliased

3 From the Limits drop down menu choose Contiguous to color pixels immediately adjacent to the pixels you drag across and that fall within the Tolerance setting. Choose Discontiguous to color pixels anywhere within the brush diameter, even if the pixels are not immediately adjacent to the pixels you drag across. Choose Find Edges to help preserve sharpness along edge detail as you replace color.

 Enter a Tolerance amount, or drag the Tolerance slider to set a Tolerance value. Set a low value to limit changes to pixels that are very similar in color to the pixels at the center of the brush. Set a high value to color a broader range of pixels:

4 Position your cursor on the pixels you want to change. The Color Replacement tool displays a crosshair at the centre of the brush cursor. This indicates the tool's "hotspot" – the point at which the tool's settings have the greatest effect. Click and drag to paint over the pixels.

Making Selections

One of the most important techniques when using Photoshop is making selections. When you make a selection, you are selecting an area of the image to which you want to make changes, and isolating the remainder of the image so that it is not affected by changes. A selection is indicated on-screen by a selection marquee – a dotted line, sometimes referred to as the "marching ants" border.

Covers

Chapter Eight

The Marquee Selection Tools

The Marquee selection tools allow you to drag with the mouse to make selections. You can make rectangular or elliptical selections by choosing the appropriate tool.

If you are working on an image with more than one layer, make sure you select the appropriate target layer before you make a selection.

1 To make a rectangular or oval selection, choose the Rectangular or Elliptical Marquee tool.

Hold down Shift, then click and drag with the Rectangular or Elliptical Marquee tool to create a square or circular selection. Hold down Alt/ option to create a selection from the center out.

2 Position your cursor on the image, then click and drag to define the area you want to select. When you release the cursor you will see a dotted rectangular or oval marquee defining the area of the selection.

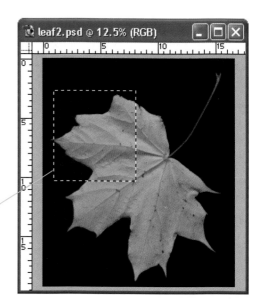

3 You can reposition the selection marquee if you need to. Make sure the Marquee tool is still selected, position your cursor inside the selection marquee (the cursor changes shape), then click and drag. You can move selection marquees with any of the Selection tools.

As you are dragging to create a selection, you can hold down the Spacebar to reposition the marquee.

4 With the Marquee tool selected, you can deselect a selection by clicking inside or outside the selection marquee. Alternatively, you can choose Select>Deselect (Command/Ctrl+D).

Marquee Options

Double-click the Rectangular or Elliptical Marquee tool to show the Options bar if it is not already showing.

You can use the Marquee Options bar to make changes to the way in which the Marquee tools work.

1 Select the Rectangular or Elliptical Marquee tool. Make sure the New Selection button is selected in the Options bar.

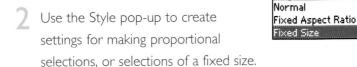

You can have only one selection active at a time, although a selection can consist of several non-contiguous areas.

2 Use the Style pop-up to create settings for making proportional selections, or selections of a fixed size.
If you select Fixed Size, enter the values you require in the Width and Height entry fields.

The Anti-aliased option is available in the Elliptical Marquee, Lasso and Magic Wand Options bars.

3 The Anti-aliased option is an important control when using bitmap applications such as Photoshop. Select Anti-aliased to create a slightly blurred, soft edge around the selection and the pixels that surround the selection. Using Anti-aliased helps avoid creating unwanted jagged edges.

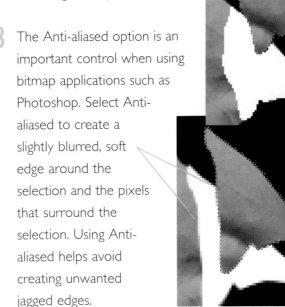

Choose Select>Reselect to reselect your most recent selection. You can use the Reselect command even if you have performed operations and commands on the image since you deselected.

4 Use the Feather entry field to create a soft, feathered edge. (See pages 106–107 in this chapter.)

Moving Selections

You can use the Selection tools to reposition a selection border, but you must use the Move tool if you want to move pixels from one location to another.

1 Make a selection. Select the Move tool, then position your cursor inside the Marquee selection border. Click and drag to move the selection.

When you move pixels on the Background layer, the area from which the pixels are moved is filled with the current background color. As long as the selection border remains selected, you can continue to move the pixels. Whilst the selection is active, the pixels in the selection "float" above the underlying pixels, without replacing them.

2 To "defloat" the pixels so that they replace the underlying pixels, choose Select>Deselect if you have the Move tool or Magic Wand tool selected. If you used Command/Ctrl with a Marquee or Lasso tool selected, click outside the selection marquee. As soon as you deselect, the pixels on the Background layer that were underneath the floating selection – the underlying pixels – are completely replaced by the pixels in the floating selection.

3 To move a selection and make a copy of it at the same time, hold down Alt/option before you drag with the Move tool. The cursor turns into a double-headed arrow, indicating that you are copying the selection.

4 You can turn a "floating" selection into a layer by choosing Layer>New>Layer Via Cut/Layer Via Copy. (See Chapter 9.)

The Lasso Tools

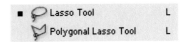

You can use the Lasso tool to make freeform selections by clicking and dragging. It is a useful tool for selecting irregular areas and for quickly adding to or subtracting from selections made with the Magic Wand tool.

Hold down Shift, then click and drag around an area to add it to the selection.
Hold down Alt/option, then click and drag around an area to remove it from the selection.

Select the Lasso tool. Set Feather and Anti-aliased options. Position your cursor on the image. The cursor changes to the Lasso cursor. Click and drag around the part of the image you want to select. Make sure your cursor comes back to the start point. If you release before reaching the start point, Photoshop completes the selection with a straight line. A dotted marquee defines the selected area.

When you return to the start point with the Polygon Lasso tool, a small circle appears at the bottom right of the cursor to indicate that you can close the selection by clicking once.

Polygon Lasso tool

The Polygon Lasso tool creates a freeform selection with straight line segments.

Select the Polygon Lasso tool. Position your cursor on the image, then click; move the cursor, then click… and so on, until you have defined the area you want to select. Click back at the start point to complete the selection. Alternatively, you can double-click to close the selection marquee.

If you have a Feather amount set in the Lasso Options bar, you will not end up with sharp corners on the selection you make.

The Magnetic Lasso tool

The Magnetic Lasso tool is most useful when you want to select an object or an area of the image which contrasts strongly with the area surrounding it.

Select the Magnetic Lasso tool. Click on the edge of the object you want to select to place the first fastening point. Either, move

the cursor along the edge of the object, or click and drag along the edge to draw a freehand segment. As you move along the edge of the object, the "active" segment of the selection border snaps to the most clearly defined edge in the image near the cursor. Fastening points are added automatically, at intervals, as you drag.

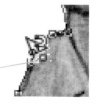

2 To close the selection border, position your cursor on the start point, (a small circle at the cursor indicates that you are on the start point) then click. Alternatively, double-click, or press the Enter/ Return key. Photoshop creates a segment from the point you have reached to the start point of the selection border. To close the selection border with a straight line segment, hold down Alt/option and double-click.

Lasso Width

The Magnetic Lasso tool detects edges only within the specified distance from the pointer. Enter a value between 1–40.

Frequency

This setting determines the rate at which fastening points are set. Enter a value between 0–100. The higher the value you set, the more frequently fastening points are placed.

Edge Contrast

Enter a value between 1–100%. This value determines how sensitive the Magnetic Lasso tool is to edges in the image. Higher values select edges that contrast strongly with their background. Lower values select edges that have smaller amounts of contrast.

The Magic Wand Tool

The Magic Wand tool selects continuous areas of color in an image, based on a Tolerance setting. Low Tolerance settings create a very limited selection of color. Higher settings select a wider range of pixels. The tool is good for selecting areas of reasonably consistent color.

To add to a selection using the Magic Wand tool, hold down Shift, then click on an unselected part of the image.

1 Before creating a selection using the Magic Wand tool, check the Tolerance setting. Double-click the Magic Wand tool to display the Magic Wand Options bar if it is not showing, or choose Window>Options to show the Options bar. Enter a Tolerance value from 0–255. If you set a tolerance value of 255, you will select every pixel in the image.

Typically, you will fine-tune Magic Wand selections using a combination of the other selection tools, together with the Grow and Similar commands.

2 Click on the image to select pixels of similar color value. All adjacent pixels that are within the Tolerance range are selected. Adjust the default setting of 32 as necessary to make the selection you require.

3 Deselect the Contiguous option to select pixels throughout the image that fall within the Tolerance setting. The result is similar to using the Similar command (see page 109).

You cannot use the Magic Wand tool in Bitmap mode.

4 To deselect a selection marquee when the Magic Wand tool is selected, click inside the selection marquee. If you click outside the selection marquee, you will create another selection based around the pixel where you clicked.

Feathering Selections

You can use the Feather option to control the degree to which the edge of a selection is softened or faded. Feathering a selection creates a transition boundary between the selection and the surrounding pixels, which can cause a loss of detail.

1. Select one of the Lasso tools, or the Elliptical Marquee selection tool. The Options bar updates according to the tool you select.

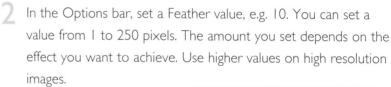

2. In the Options bar, set a Feather value, e.g. 10. You can set a value from 1 to 250 pixels. The amount you set depends on the effect you want to achieve. Use higher values on high resolution images.

3. Create a selection using either the Marquee or Lasso tool. When you move the selection you will see the feathered edge around the selection and also where you move the selection from.

4. Alternatively, using any of the selection tools, you can make a selection and then choose Select> Feather. Enter a value in the Feather Radius box.

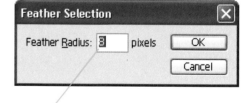

Creating a vignette

You can use the feathering option to create a vignette effect – a soft, fading edge to an image.

1   Before you begin, make sure your background color is set to white (see Chapter Five – "Defining Colors"). Then set a Feather value in the Options bar for the selection tool you are using.

If you set a feather amount for a tool, it's a good idea to reset the Feather field back to zero immediately after you finish using the tool. If you don't, you may find that these settings come back to haunt you at a later stage.

2   Next, create a selection, which can be a regular or irregular shape.

3   Choose Select>Inverse. This reverses the selection – selecting all the pixels that were previously not selected.

Feathering, unlike anti-aliasing, blurs the inside and outside of a selection boundary.

4   Press Delete (Mac) or Backspace (Windows) to delete the area surrounding your selection, leaving a feathered edge.

Modifying Selections

There are many instances when you need to add to or subtract from a selection. You can use any combination of selection tools to make the selection you want. For example, you might start by making a selection with the Magic Wand tool, then add to the selection using the Lasso tool.

1 To add to an existing selection, hold down the Shift key, then click and drag to create another selection marquee that intersects the existing selection marquee.

2 You can use the same technique to create non-adjoining selections. Although the selections may be in different parts of the image, they count and act as one selection. For example, if you apply a filter, the effect will be apparent in all the selection marquees.

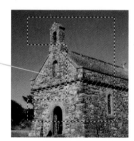

3 To add to a selection, hold down Shift and use the Lasso tool to quickly loop around small areas that the Magic Wand tool typically misses out from its selection.

4 To subtract from a selection, hold down Alt/option, then click and drag with a selection tool to intersect the existing selection marquee. The area defined by the intersecting marquee will be removed from the original selection.

The Grow and Similar Commands

The Grow and Similar commands are very useful when used in conjunction with the Magic Wand tool to add to a selection. Both work according to the Tolerance setting set in the Magic Wand Options bar.

If necessary, change the Tolerance setting for the Magic Wand tool before using the Grow command to achieve a more, or less inclusive result.

The Grow command selects contiguous or adjoining areas of color based on the Tolerance setting in the Magic Wand Options bar.

1 Make a selection. Check that the Tolerance setting in the Magic Wand Options bar is appropriate.

2 Choose Select>Grow. Pixels which fall within the Tolerance setting and are adjacent to pixels already in the selection are added to the selection.

The Similar command selects non-adjacent pixels that fall within the same Tolerance setting as set in the Magic Wand Options bar.

Using the Magic Wand tool, with the Contiguous option (in the Options bar) deselected, is the equivalent of using the Similar command.

1 Make a selection using any of the selection tools. Check that the Tolerance setting in the Magic Wand Options bar is appropriate.

2 Choose Select>Similar. Pixels throughout the image that fall within the Tolerance setting are selected.

Pasting Into Selections

Pasting into selections is useful for compositing images.

When you paste into a selection, the selection from the Clipboard will be rendered at the resolution of the destination document. This means that the selection from the source document will change size if the resolution of the two documents is different.

1 Create a selection in the destination window.

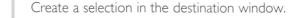
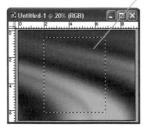

2 Open the source document, then make the selection you want to paste into the destination document. Choose Edit>Copy to copy the selection to the Clipboard.

3 Click in the destination image window. The selection should still be active. Choose Edit>Paste Into (Command/Ctrl+Shift+V) to paste the Clipboard selection into the selected area.

Make sure the layer mask is selected, then paint with black to add to the mask, or paint with white to subtract from the mask. (See pages 160–161, "Layer Masks".)

4 Use the Move tool to reposition the pasted selection relative to the original selection.

5 The Paste Into command creates a layer mask. The layer is active, indicated by the Paintbrush icon in the Layers palette, which means that you can edit the layer. To edit the mask, click the Mask icon in the Layers palette. A small circle replaces the paintbrush, indicating that the layer mask is selected.

The Defringe Command

You can drag a selection from one window to another image window. This is useful when creating a composite image. Defringe is useful when you use this technique, as it helps to blend the selection into its new environment.

1. To drag a selection from one image window to another, first make a selection in the source window. Select the Move tool, position the Move cursor inside the selection, then click and drag into the destination window.

2. When you release the mouse button, the selection appears in the destination window on a new layer. The destination window becomes the active window, and the new layer is the active layer. Check to see if there are unwanted pixels causing a halo effect around the edge of the selection.

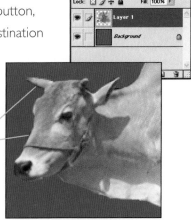

A width setting of 1 or 2 pixels is usually sufficient to defringe a pasted or moved selection.

3. To defringe the moved selection, make sure the newly created layer is active. Choose Layer> Matting>Defringe. Enter a value for the Width then OK the dialog box. The selection should now blend in better.

Filling a Selection

You can use the Fill dialog box in order to fill an entire layer or a selection.

1. To fill a selection, first define either a foreground or background color that you want to fill with, then make a selection. Choose Edit>Fill. Use the Use pop-up to choose the fill type. You can also set Opacity for the fill and a Blending Mode. Click OK.

See pages 82–84 for a description of the blending modes.

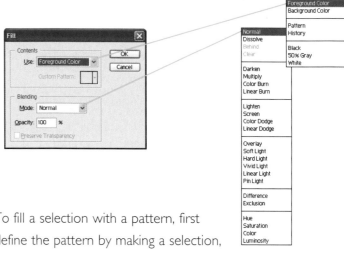

2. To fill a selection with a pattern, first define the pattern by making a selection, then choosing Edit>Define Pattern.

3. Make the selection you want to fill with the previously defined pattern.

4. Choose Edit>Fill. Choose Pattern from the Contents pop-up. Use the Custom Pattern pop-up menu to choose the pattern. OK the dialog box to fill the selection with the pattern.

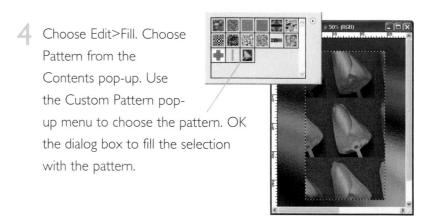

Copying and Pasting Selections

You can use the Clipboard to copy and paste selections within the same image and into other images.

A useful technique for selecting a simple image, like the runner on this page, is the Inverse selection command. Use the Magic Wand tool to select the background, then choose Select>Inverse to reverse the selection. The areas that represent the runner are now selected.

1 To copy a selection, first make a selection using any of the selection tools. Choose Edit>Copy.

2 To paste the selection into the same image, choose Edit>Paste. The selection is pasted into the image on its own layer. (For information on working with layers, see Chapter Nine, "Layers".)

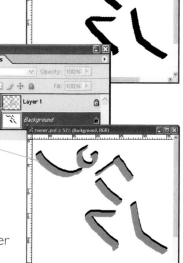

3 To paste the selection into another image, click on the other image window if it is already open, or use File>Open to open another image. Choose Edit>Paste to paste the selection from the Clipboard onto a new layer in the active image.

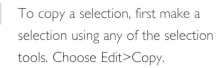

Use the Defringe command (see page 111) to help a pasted or dragged selection blend into its new surroundings.

4 You can also drag a selection from one image window into another. You need two image windows open – the source and the destination windows. Make a selection in the source window, select the Move tool, position your cursor within the selection, then click and drag into the destination window. The selection appears on its own layer.

Transforming Selections

The ability to transform a selection's bounding box enables you to fine tune selections, distort selections and make selections that were previously difficult to achieve.

The Transform Selection bounding box transforms the selection border only. It does not transform the pixels within the selection.

1 To transform a selection, choose Select>Transform Selection. A bounding box with eight handles appears around the selection. A Point of Origin marker appears at the center of the bounding box.

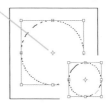

2 To scale a selection, click and drag a handle. The cursor becomes a bidirectional arrow. To scale a selection in proportion, hold down Shift then drag a handle.

Drag the Point of Origin to a new location to specify the point around which transformations take place.

3 To rotate a selection, position your cursor just outside the selection border. The cursor changes to a bi-directional, curved arrow. Click and drag in a circular direction.

4 To distort the selection boundary, hold down Command/Ctrl then drag a corner handle.

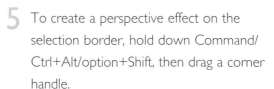

5 To create a perspective effect on the selection border, hold down Command/Ctrl+Alt/option+Shift, then drag a corner handle.

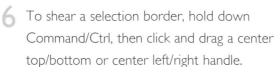

6 To shear a selection border, hold down Command/Ctrl, then click and drag a center top/bottom or center left/right handle.

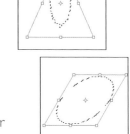

You can also double-click inside the transform bounding box to accept the transformation.

7 Click the Cancel button in the Options bar, or press the Esc key to remove the transform bounding box without applying the changes. Click the Commit button or press Return/Enter to apply the transformation.

Layers

Layers introduce a considerable degree of flexibility into the way in which you can work with images. Layers let you keep various image elements separate so that you can make changes without deleting or changing the underlying pixels.

Each additional layer you create increases the file size of the image. You can selectively merge layers into each other to help manage and consolidate layers as you work. When you have finished editing your image, you can flatten the image to merge all layers into a single Background layer. You will need to do this to use your image in QuarkXPress. You should note that you can only save images with layers in Photoshop and TIFF file formats.

Covers

Chapter Nine

Working with Layers

When you create or open an image for the first time, it consists of one default layer called Background.

New layers are automatically created when you use the Type tool to add text to an image, when you drag or copy a selection into an image, and also when you drag a layer from one document into another.

To edit layer options for a layer after you have created it, choose Layer Properties from the palette menu.

One of the most useful techniques for creating a new layer is to make a selection on a part of the Background layer, then choose Layer>New>Layer via Copy (Command/Ctrl+J). The selection of pixels is copied to a new layer. You can now edit and transform the pixels on the new layer with the original pixels intact on the Background layer.

To access the Layers palette, choose Window>Layers.

1 To create a new layer, choose New Layer from the palette menu. Enter a name for the new layer in the dialog box. You can also choose Opacity and Blending Mode settings at this stage if you want to.

2 Alternatively, click once on the New Layer icon at the bottom of the Layers palette.

3 OK the dialog box, or press Return/Enter. The new layer appears in the Layers palette above the previously highlighted layer. Notice also that the file size in the Document Sizes status bar area increases when you paint on or add pixels to the layer.

4 To rename a layer, position your cursor on the layer's label, then double-click. Enter a new name in the label entry area, then press Enter/Return on the keyboard.

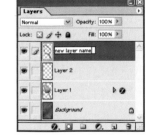

5 To delete a layer, click on the layer to select it. Then choose Delete Layer from the palette menu. Click Yes or No in the Delete Layer warning box. Alternatively, drag the Layer name onto the Wastebasket icon at the bottom of the Layers palette. No warning alert appears if you use this method.

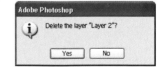

Selecting, hiding and showing layers

You can only work on one layer at a time. This is often referred to as the "target" or active layer.

You can also click the Eye icon to hide/show a layer set and a layer style.

1 Click on the layer name in the Layers palette to make it active. The layer name highlights and the Paintbrush icon appears in the second column on the left of the palette. The name of the active layer appears in the title bar of the image window.

tupilpbg.psd @ 100% (outline, RGB)

To select all pixels on a layer, hold down Command/Ctrl and click on the layer name in the Layers palette.

2 To hide a layer, click on the Eye icon in the leftmost column of the Layers palette. To show a layer, click in the leftmost column to bring back the Eye icon.

Reordering layers

It is often necessary to reorder the stacking position of layers to control which layers appear in front of other layers.

You can move pixels in a layer beyond the edge of your picture. These non-visible pixels will be saved with the document. Non-visible pixels are lost when you flatten the image.

1 To change the layering order, click and drag the layer name you want to reposition. Notice the horizontal bar that appears as you move the layer upwards or downwards. Release the mouse when the horizontal bar appears in the position to which you want the layer moved.

Repositioning layer contents

You can reposition the entire contents of a layer using the Move tool.

You can nudge the contents of a selected layer in 1-pixel increments by pressing the arrow keys when the Move tool is selected.

1 Click on the layer you want to move in the Layers palette. Select the Move tool, then position your cursor anywhere on the image. Click and drag to move the layer.

Merging and Flattening Layers

Use the Merge commands to combine two or more layers into one layer. This is useful for keeping the file size down and for consolidating elements on different layers into a single manageable layer or unit.

The Merge Visible Layers command in the palette menu merges only the currently visible layers.

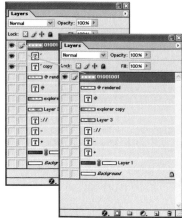

To merge all the visible layers in your document, first hide any layers you don't want to merge. Make sure one of the layers you want to merge is active, then choose Merge Visible from the palette menu, or choose Layer> Merge Visible.

When you use the Flatten Image command, any hidden layers will be discarded.

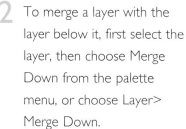

To merge a layer with the layer below it, first select the layer, then choose Merge Down from the palette menu, or choose Layer> Merge Down.

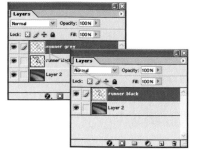

When you convert images between some modes you are prompted to flatten the file. Make sure you save a copy of the file first if you want to be able to go back and make further changes to the layers.

Flattening images

When you flatten an image, you end up with a Background layer only. This reduces the file size. Flatten an image when you have finished creating and positioning the elements of your composite image, and are ready to save the file in a suitable format for placing in a page layout application.

To flatten an image, make sure that all the layers you want to keep are visible. Choose Flatten Image from the Layers palette menu, or choose Layers>Flatten Image.

Moving Layers Between Images

The layer you move into the destination image window is rendered at the resolution of the destination window. This may cause the elements on the moved layer to appear larger or smaller than in the original window. To avoid surprises, make sure that the source and destination images are at the same resolution.

Also, if the modes of the two images are different, the layer you move will be converted to match the mode of the destination window.

You can copy a complete layer from one Photoshop document to another, similar to the way you move a selection from one document to another.

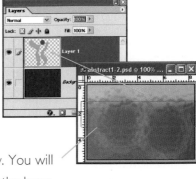

1 First make sure you have two document windows open — a "source" document and a "destination" document. The source document contains the layer you want to copy. The destination document is the document into which you want to copy the layer.

2 Click in the source document window to make it active. Position your cursor on the layer in the Layers palette, then drag the layer you want to copy from the source document into the destination document window. You will see a bounding box indicating the layer you are copying.

Use the Defringe command (see page 111) to remove any fringe around pixels on a layer that you copy from one image to another.

3 Position the layer and then release the mouse. The layer is positioned above the previously active layer in the destination document's Layers palette. The destination document is now the active image window.

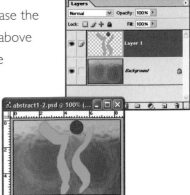

Linking Layers

Linking layers is useful when you want to keep elements of an image on separate layers, but you need to move the layers maintaining the exact positional relationship of each.

1 To move the foreground object with its shadow (which is on a separate layer), show the Layers palette (Window>Layers) and make sure that one of the layers you want to link is active.

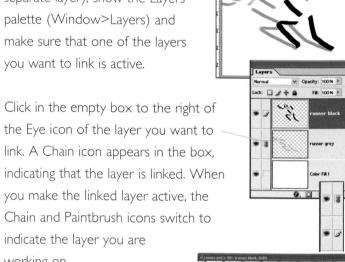

The principle of linking layers works, even if the layers are not next to each other in the Layers palette.

2 Click in the empty box to the right of the Eye icon of the layer you want to link. A Chain icon appears in the box, indicating that the layer is linked. When you make the linked layer active, the Chain and Paintbrush icons switch to indicate the layer you are working on.

3 Use the Move tool to reposition the elements on the linked layers as one.

4 You can link multiple layers using the same technique.

5 To unlink a layer, click the Chain icon. The layer is now completely independent again.

Adjustment Layers

Using an adjustment layer is like positioning a lens above the pixels on the layers below it to change their appearance. If you don't like the result, you can edit the adjustment layer to achieve the result you want, or you can discard the adjustment layer. When you are satisfied with the result you can implement the adjustment layer as a permanent change.

1 Select a layer in the Layers palette. The adjustment layer will be positioned above the currently active layer. Choose Layer>New Adjustment Layer.

2 Choose a type from the New Adjustment Layer sub-menu. This automatically becomes the name for the layer. Enter a different name if desired. Set Opacity and Blending Mode at this stage if you want to. Click OK.

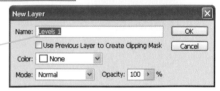

3 Depending on the type of adjustment layer you chose, the appropriate dialog box opens. Create the settings you want to experiment with. OK the dialog box.

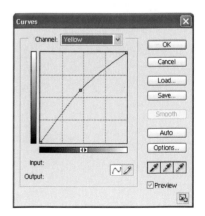

4 The new adjustment layer appears in the Layers palette as the active layer. The settings you created are now applied to all layers below the adjustment layer.

5 Click the Eye icon to hide/show the preview of the changes brought about by the adjustment layer settings. Double-click the adjustment layer to re-enter the appropriate adjustment dialog box to make changes to the settings.

The adjustment layer settings do not have a permanent effect on pixels until the layer is merged with other layers, or the image is flattened.

6 Drag the adjustment layer into the Wastebasket if you want to discard the settings.

7 When you are ready to make the settings of the adjustment layer permanent, either use one of the Merge commands from the palette menu, or flatten the image.

Locking Layers

There are four levels of lock that can be applied to layers. A dimmed lock icon appears to the right of the layer when you select one of the lock options. A solid lock icon appears when the layer is fully locked.

The Background layer is automatically fully locked by default.

Transparent areas on a layer are indicated by the checkerboard pattern when the Background layer is hidden.

You can move locked layers to a new position in the stacking order of layers, but you cannot delete a fully locked layer.

Select a linked layer, then select the Lock All option to lock all properties for the linked layers.

The Lock Transparency and Lock Image Pixels options are automatically selected for Type layers you create. You cannot turn these options off.

1 To completely lock a layer, select the layer in the Layers palette, then click the Lock All option. You will not be able to reposition the layer or make any changes to it, including changing blending mode, opacity and layer style.

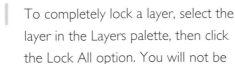

2 To prevent the layer from being moved using the Move tool, click the Lock Position option.

3 To disable painting tools on the layer, select the Lock Image pixels option. You can still edit any mask applied to the layer. You cannot move the layer. Selecting the Lock Image pixels option automatically locks transparency for the layer.

4 Click Lock Transparency to preserve transparent areas of a layer. You can make changes to the existing pixels on the layer, but you cannot make changes to any areas of transparency. For example, if Lock Transparency is selected, the blur filters do not work effectively on the layer as blurred pixels cannot be spread into the areas of transparency.

Layer Sets

When you create complex images with multiple layers it is convenient to simplify the layers palette by grouping related layers together into a layer set. Creating layer sets in complex, multi-layered images makes it much easier to manage the elements in the image.

1. To create a new layer set, click the New Layer Set button in the bottom of the Layers palette to use the current default settings, or choose New Layer Set from the palette menu.

2. To create a layer set from existing layers, first link the layers you want to combine into a layer set. Choose New Set From Linked in the palette menu, or choose Layer>New>Layer Set from Linked.

3. To move a layer into a layer set, drag a layer onto the Layer Set folder. Release the mouse when the Layer Set folder highlights. The layer is positioned at the bottom of the layers already in the layer set. If the layer set is expanded, drag the layer to the desired position. Release when the highlight bar is in the correct position.

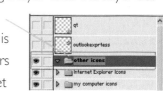

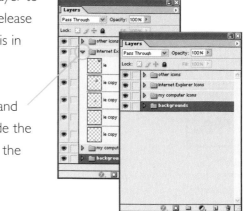

4. Click the Collapse/Expand triangle to reveal or hide the layers contained within the layer set.

Layer Styles

Using the Layer Style sub-menu, you can create sophisticated layer effects such as soft shadows, beveled and embossed edges, and inner and outer glows quickly and easily. This example consists of 3 layers – a white Background layer, a colored circle Shape layer and a colored triangle Shape layer, and uses Bevel and Emboss options to demonstrate the principles for creating a layer style.

Each layer style provides a range of options specific to that style. Experiment with the options to achieve the effect you want.

In the Layer Style dialog box, make sure the Preview option is selected to see the effect applied in the image.

You cannot apply a layer style to the Background layer, a layer set or a locked layer.

You can also select a layer style option using the Add Layer Style button (🄵.) at the bottom of the Layers palette.

1 To apply a layer style, click on a layer in the Layers palette to make it active. Choose Layer>Layer Style>Bevel & Emboss.

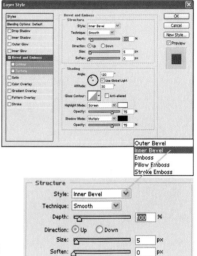

2 In the Structure section, choose a style from the Style pop-up menu and a technique from the Technique pop-up menu. Select the Up/Down radio button to light the effect from above or below.

3 Use the Depth entry box or slider to adjust the height of the effect. Use the Size slider to control the spread of the bevel. The Soften slider controls the overall intensity of the effect and helps reduce irregularities or artifacts in the effect, creating a smoother result.

4 In the Shading area, enter a value in the Angle entry box to control the direction of the light source. Enter a value in the Altitude entry box to define the apparent depth of the light source. Drag in the Angle/Altitude disk to create settings manually if you prefer.

5 Gloss Contour allows you to change the transition of the effect across the affected pixels on the layer.

6 Adjust settings for the Highlight and Shadow edges of the effect. It is a good idea initially to leave the blending modes set to Screen and Multiply respectively. Experiment with the Opacity sliders to create a more subtle effect.

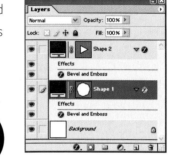

7 OK the dialog when you are satisfied with the results. Notice in the Layers palette a "f" symbol ( ) on the layer, indicating that there is a layer effect applied to the layer. Whilst the "f" symbol appears the layer effect remains editable.

Click on the Expand/Collapse triangle ( ) to hide or show the layer styles applied to a layer.

Managing Layer Styles

Once you have created a layer effect you can continue to edit the effect and you can use a variety of commands from the Layer Effects sub-menu to manage the effects.

1 To edit the layer effect settings, select the layer, then click the Expand triangle to display layer effects as separate entries in the Layers palette. Double-click the "f" icon next to the name of the effect. You can continue to adjust settings as long as the layer displays the Layer Effects icon.

To temporarily disable layer effects on all layers, not just the active layer, choose Layer>Layer Style>Hide All Effects. Choose Layer>Layer Style>Show All Effects to reverse the process.

2 To keep the angle of the light source constant if you are using layer effects on more than one layer in an image, choose Layer>Layer Style>Global Light. Enter a value for the Angle in the Global Angle entry box. OK the dialog box. Make sure you select the Use Global Light option when you create multiple layer effects in the Layer Style dialog box.

3 To copy exact layer effect settings from one layer to another, first select a layer with a layer effect applied to it, then choose Copy Layer Style from the Layer Style sub-menu. Click on another layer in the Layers palette. Choose Paste Layer Style from the Layer Style sub-menu.

Once you merge a layer with a layer effect applied to it, you can no longer adjust the layer effect settings.

4 To permanently remove layer styles from a layer, make sure you select the appropriate layer, then choose Layer>Layer Style>Clear Layer Styles.

5 Layer styles automate procedures that in the past you had to perform yourself. Use the Create Layer command from the Layer Styles sub-menu to separate the layer effect into the multiple layers that Photoshop uses to create the effect. This can be useful if you need to edit specific parts of the effect.

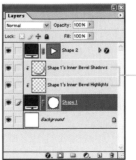

Transforming Layers

You cannot transform the Background layer in an image.

An advantage of using Free Transform is that you can make multiple transformations, then either accept or discard the result.

To use Perspective and Distort transformations on a Type layer, you must first render (convert to pixels) the Type layer – Layer>Type>Render Layer.

Position your cursor inside the bounding box, then click and drag, to reposition the layer whilst the transformation bounding box is still active.

The Transform sub-menu (Edit> Transform) gives alternative options for transforming layers.

Once you have moved pixels to a new layer you can then transform the layer. Using Free Transform you can scale, rotate, distort, skew and create perspective effects.

1 Ensure the layer is active. Choose Edit>Free Transform. A bounding box with handles appears around the pixels. To scale a layer, drag a handle. To scale in proportion, hold down Shift then drag a corner handle.

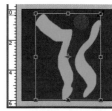

2 To rotate a layer, position your cursor slightly outside the bounding box. The cursor changes to a bi-directional arrow. Drag in a circular direction. You can drag the Point of Origin marker to a new position to specify the point around which the rotation takes place.

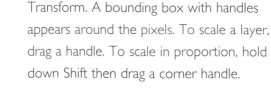

3 To skew the layer, hold down Command/ Ctrl+Shift, then drag the center top/bottom, or the center left/right handle.

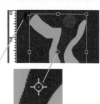

4 To create perspective, hold down Command/Ctrl+Alt/option+Shift then drag a corner handle. To distort the layer, hold down Command/Ctrl then drag a corner handle. This allows you to move corner handles independently.

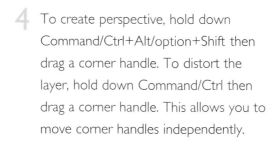
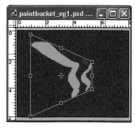

5 Click the Cancel button in the Options bar, or press Esc to revert to the original state without making changes. Click the Commit button or press Return/Enter to accept the transformation and remove the Transformation bounding box.

New Layer Commands

The New Layer via Cut (Command/Ctrl+Shift+J) and the New Layer via Copy (Command/Ctrl+J) commands are essential options when creating layers. Use these commands to either cut or copy selected pixels to a new layer.

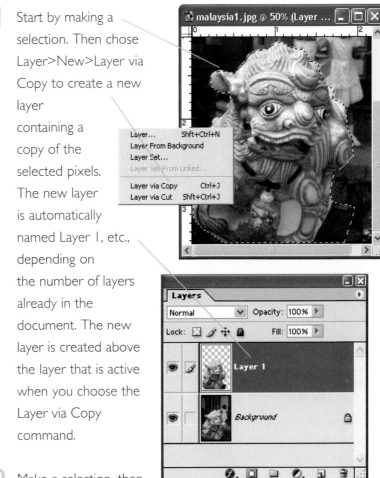

1 Start by making a selection. Then chose Layer>New>Layer via Copy to create a new layer containing a copy of the selected pixels. The new layer is automatically named Layer 1, etc., depending on the number of layers already in the document. The new layer is created above the layer that is active when you choose the Layer via Copy command.

2 Make a selection, then choose New Layer via Cut to cut the selected pixels to a new layer. Notice when you reposition the pixels on the new layer, the area on the Background layer from which they were cut is filled with the current background color.

Layer Comps

Layer comps make it easy to return to a particular arrangement of an image and to experiment freely with different compositions within the same image.

A layer comp is a snapshot of an image that records the visibility and position of layers, and any layer styles for an image at a particular point in time. Layer comps provide a convenient means for recording various permutations of image layers without having to create multiple, separate image files. Unlike Snapshots created in the History palette, Layer comps are saved with the file.

See page 27 for information on working with palettes in the Palette Well.

1 On launching Photoshop, the Layer Comps palette is docked in the Palette Well in the Options bar. Click the Layer Comps tab to work with the palette from the dock.

2 Create the arrangement and visibility settings for the layer palette that you want to record, then either click the Create New Layer Comp button () at the bottom of the palette, or choose New Layer Comp from the palette menu.

Position your cursor on the Layer Comp tab in the Palette Well, then drag into the Photoshop working area to create a floating palette. Choose Dock to Palette Well from the Layer Comps palette menu if you want to move the palette back to the Palette Well.

3 In the New Layer Comp dialog box, enter a name for the Layer Comp. Select Visibility, Position and Appearance options that you want to record in the Layer Comp.

4 Add an additional explanatory note in the Comment entry box if required.

Settings you create in the New Layer Comp dialog box become the defaults for the next time you use the dialog box.

5 Click OK. The New Layer Comp is added at the bottom of the Layer Comps palette, below any existing Layer Comps.

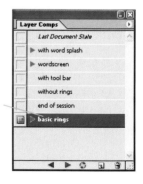

Viewing and Managing Layer Comps

Layer Comps add flexibility and a degree of complexity to the way in which you work with and manage images. You should be careful about the way you manage layer comp variations in order to work effectively, smoothly and productively.

Always experiment on a copy of your image when you begin working with a new feature such as Layer Comps so that you don't unintentionally loose any work you have already done that you might want to keep.

1 To change the name of a layer comp, double-click the layer comp name in the Layer Comp palette to highlight the existing name. Enter a new name then press Return/Enter.

2 To change the layer comp settings you selected when you first created the layer comp, double-click the layer comp entry line (but not directly on the layer comp name) to access the Layer Comp Options dialog box. Make changes as required.

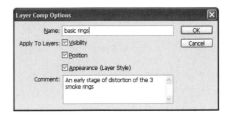

The Last Document State entry is always displayed at the top of the Layer Comp palette.

3 To display a layer comp in the image window, either click in the Apply Layer Comp box to the left of the layer comp name, or click the Apply Previous/Next Selected Layer Comp arrow button at the bottom of the palette.

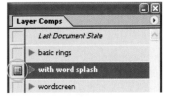

You cannot click the Apply Next/ Previous Selected Layer Comp arrow button to move to Last Document State of the image.

4 Click the Apply Last Document State box, or choose Restore Last Document State from the palette menu to return to the state of the document you are currently working on.

5 If you make changes to a layer, for example, deleting a layer that is already recorded as an element in a Layer Comp, a warning triangle appears to the right of all layer comps that are affected. You can update the layer comp with the new settings by selecting the layer comp, then clicking the Update Layer Comp button, or choosing Update Layer Comp from the palette menu.

Layer Comps add to the file size of an image. It is a good idea to delete at least some of your layer comps when they are no longer required.

6 To delete a layer comp, click on it to select it, then click the Wastebasket icon at the bottom of the palette, or drag the layer comp into the Wastebasket. There is no warning message when you delete a layer comp. Use the History palette if necessary to restore a deleted layer comp.

Working with Type

You can create and edit type directly in the image window. The type you create is preserved as vector outlines or paths which means that Photoshop can output type with sharp, resolution-independent edges.

The Masked Type option allows you to create complex selections in the shape of type characters.

You can choose different alignments vertically and horizontally for type, you can rotate it, fill it with a gradient, pattern or image, create translucent type and much more.

Covers

Chapter Ten

Creating Point Type

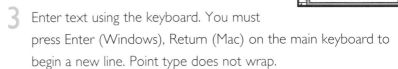
T Horizontal Type Tool   T

You can create two kinds of type: Point type and Paragraph type. Typically, you use Point type when you want to work with small amounts of text, such as a single character, word, or line. Use Paragraph type when you are working with more extensive blocks of type in paragraphs.

The small bar running through the bottom of the I-beam cursor indicates the position of the type's baseline.

To create Point type, select the Horizontal Type tool (T). You can create settings for the type using options in the Options bar, or the Character and Paragraph palettes, before you enter the type, or you can format the type after you enter it.

You can also commit type by pressing the Enter key on the numeric keypad, or choosing any other tool in the Toolbox.

Position your cursor in the image window, then click to place the text insertion point. Clicking with the Horizontal Type tool takes Photoshop into Text Editing mode.

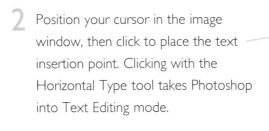

You must be in Text Editing mode to enter, edit or format text.

Enter text using the keyboard. You must press Enter (Windows), Return (Mac) on the main keyboard to begin a new line. Point type does not wrap.

Click on the Commit button in the Options bar when you have finished entering or editing type to commit the Type layer. This takes Photoshop out of Text Editing mode and you can now perform other tasks on the image. The type appears on its own layer. Click the Cancel button to discard the type.

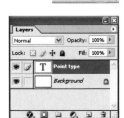

For images in Multichannel, Bitmap or Indexed Color mode, type does not appear on its own layer, it appears as pixels on the Background layer and cannot be edited.

The Options bar with the Type tool selected

The Options bar in Text Editing mode

Creating Paragraph Type

When you work with Paragraph type, you define the width of the column of text. The text wraps to a new line when it reaches the edge of the type bounding box.

1. To create Paragraph type, select the Horizontal Type tool (T). You can create settings for the type using options in the Options bar, or the Character and Paragraph palettes before you enter the type, or you can format the type after you enter it.

If you enter more type than can fit in the type bounding box, an overflow symbol appears in the bottom right corner of the bounding box:

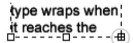

Make the type smaller, or the box bigger to see all the type.

2. Position your cursor at one corner of the type area you want to create. Drag diagonally to define the size of the type's bounding box.

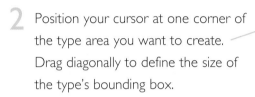

3. With the Horizontal Type tool selected, you can hold down Alt/ option, then click in the image to access the Paragraph Text Size dialog box. Enter values for Width and Height, then click OK.

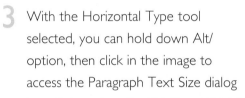

To resize the type bounding box, select the Horizontal Type tool, click on the Type layer in the Layers palette, then click in the text itself. Drag a resize handle to change the size of the text area.

4. Enter text using the keyboard. Text wraps when it reaches the edge of the type bounding box. Press Enter/Return on the main keyboard only when you want to begin a new paragraph.

5. Click on the Commit button in the Options bar to accept the Type layer. Or click the Cancel button to abandon changes. Both buttons take Photoshop out of Text Editing mode and you can now perform other tasks on the image. The type appears on its own layer.

Editing and Selecting Type

To edit type you must go into Text Editing mode. To make changes to the character/paragraph formatting of text you must first highlight or select the text on which you want to work. You can then make changes.

If you have any difficulty placing the text insertion point in the text you want to edit, click on the type layer in the Layers palette to activate the layer first.

Editing text

To edit text select the Horizontal Type tool (T). Click directly into the text you want to change. This takes Photoshop into Text Editing mode. Make changes using the keyboard as necessary. Click the Commit button in the Options bar to accept the changes you make and to leave Text Editing mode. Click the Cancel button in the Options bar if you do not want to keep the changes.

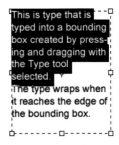

Editable Type layers are represented by the "T" icon in the Layers palette. Double-click the "T" icon to select all the text on a Type layer.

Selecting text

Make sure you are in Text Editing mode, then click and drag across the text to highlight a specific range of characters, from a single character to a word to all visible text. Double-click on a word to highlight one word. Triple-click to highlight a line of text. Click four times to select a paragraph.

To reposition type, select the Move tool, make sure the Type layer is selected in the Layers palette, then drag the Type layer as you would to reposition any other layer.

2 In Text Editing mode, use Command/Ctrl+A to select all text on the layer, or choose Select>All.

3 With the appropriate range of text highlighted you can then make changes to the settings. The changes you make apply to the highlighted text only.

Character Settings

You can choose Window> Character to show the Character/ Paragraph palette, or you can click the Palettes button in the Options bar if you have the Type tool selected.

You can use options in the Options bar when the Type tool is selected, or in the Character palette to change the settings for selected text.

Font

Use the Font pop-up to choose from the list of fonts available on your system. Choose a style – such as Bold or Italic – from the Font Style pop-up.

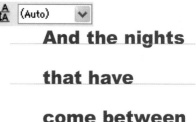

Size

Enter a value in the Size box to change the size of your type. Points are the default unit of measurement for type in Photoshop.

Make sure you have selected a range of text before you make changes to Character settings.

Leading

Leading controls the distance from one baseline of type to the next. Enter a leading value in points in the Leading entry box. Photoshop applies a default leading value of 120% of the type size you have selected if you leave the leading set to (Auto).

And the nights

that have

come between

If you are uncertain about which control is which in the Character palette, rest your cursor on the icon to the left of the entry box until the ToolTip label appears:

Kerning and tracking

In the Character palette, you can create settings for kerning and tracking. Metrics, the default, uses the built-in pair kerning table for the font.

To kern character pairs, click between the characters in the text to place the text insertion bar. You can enter a value in the Kerning entry box or use the pop-up to choose a preset value. Negative values move characters closer together. Positive values move characters apart. Press Enter/ Return to accept the changes made in the dialog.

A Faux (or false) style allows you to simulate a font style which doesn't exist on your system. You cannot apply Faux Bold to warped type.

To change the color of selected text, click the Color box in the Options bar or in the Character palette. (See pages 66–67 for further information on using the Color Picker palette.)

2 For Tracking, highlight a range of text you want to track. Enter a value in the Tracking entry box, or use the pop-up.

AWAY   Tracking = 84

AWAY   Tracking = -36

Baseline Shift

The Baseline Shift control allows you to move highlighted characters above or below their original baseline to create a variety of effects.

You must commit changes to type before you are able to make other changes to the image.

1 To baseline-shift characters, in Text Editing mode make sure you highlight the characters you want to shift.

2 Enter a positive value to baseline-shift upwards, enter a negative value to baseline-shift downward.

It's a T Y P E

Anti-aliasing

In most instances, fractional character widths provide the best spacing for type. Switch off the Fractional Widths option when working with type below 20 points that is to be viewed on screen. If you leave the option selected, type characters may run together when displayed on a monitor screen.

   Access the Fractional Widths option from the Character palette menu.

The anti-aliased setting in the Options bar creates type with a slightly soft edge. It does this by blurring the pixels that form the edge of the type. Use this option to avoid unnecessary jagged edges, unless you are working with very small type. Anti-aliasing text can help the type to blend into its background. Text that is not anti-aliased can look jagged. Choose an amount of anti-aliasing from the Anti-alias pop-up in the Options bar.

Type at very small sizes can appear blurred if anti-aliasing is applied.

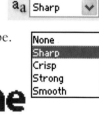

None
Sharp
Crisp
Strong
Smooth

Paragraph Settings

The controls in the Paragraph palette are most useful when you are working with Paragraph type consisting of one or more paragraphs. Choose Window>Paragraph if the palette is not already showing.

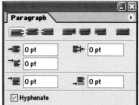

With the Type tool selected, you can click the Palettes button in the Options bar to show the Paragraph palette.

Before you can apply Paragraph settings you must highlight the range of text on which you want to work. (See page 136.)

Alignment

Select the Type layer in the Layers palette to apply settings to all paragraphs on that layer.

To change the alignment for selected paragraphs, or a complete layer, click on one of the alignment buttons: Left, Right, Center, in the Paragraph palette or Options bar.

2 Choose one of the Justify alignment options to justify type so that both edges of the column are straight. You cannot justify Point type. The variations for justified type affect how the last line of a paragraph is treated. Rest the cursor on the icon for a ToolTip label.

Indents

To set a Left, Right or First Line indent for selected paragraphs, enter a value in the appropriate entry box.

Space Before, Space After

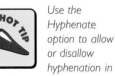

Use the Hyphenate option to allow or disallow hyphenation in selected text.

To create additional space above and/or below a paragraph or range of selected paragraphs, enter a value in the Space Before and/or Space After entry boxes.

Masked Type

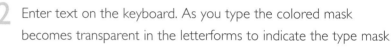

In essence, the Masked Type option creates a complex selection – a selection in the shape of type. This can be powerful and flexible when you want to show images through the shape of letterforms.

Before you commit it, you can highlight, format and move mask type as you would standard type .

Select the Type Mask tool. Position your cursor on the image where you want the type to start. Click. This sets the text insertion point. A translucent color mask appears across the image.

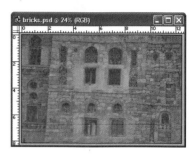

After you commit the type mask selection, use one of the selection tools to reposition the selection if necessary.

Enter text on the keyboard. As you type the colored mask becomes transparent in the letterforms to indicate the type mask selection. Click the Commit button in the Options bar to create the selection.

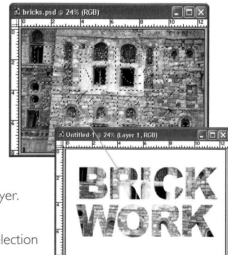

A type selection appears in the image window. Notice that the Type Mask tool does not create a new layer.

The Masked Type option creates a selection. You can move, copy, fill or stroke the masked type selection as you can for any other selection.

You can now drag the selection to a new image window, create a new layer from the selection or use any commands that you would typically use on a selection.

Type and Layer Styles

Layer styles can be applied to type layers whilst the type layer remains an editable type layer.

1 To apply a Layer Style to a type layer, first click on the type layer to make it active.

2 Choose Layer>Layer Styles. Select a style from the style sub-menu. Create settings in the Layer Style dialog box. When you OK the dialog box, the layer in the Layers palette now has a "T" and a "f" icon indicating that it is an editable type layer with a layer effect applied. (See page 125 for information on working with layer styles. See page 136 for information on working with editable type layers.)

The editable type layer with its layer style separated from the Background layer.

Type Effects

Photoshop provides a variety of creative techniques for producing interesting effects with type.

See Chapter 11 – "Paths" for information on creating paths and working with the Pen and Shape tools.

Type on a path

You can create type that follows a path created using the Pen tool or a Shape tool.

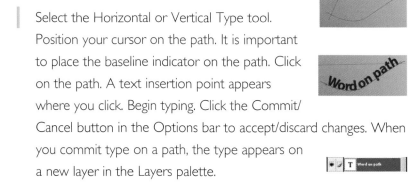

1. Select the Horizontal or Vertical Type tool. Position your cursor on the path. It is important to place the baseline indicator on the path. Click on the path. A text insertion point appears where you click. Begin typing. Click the Commit/Cancel button in the Options bar to accept/discard changes. When you commit type on a path, the type appears on a new layer in the Layers palette.

The baseline indicator is the squiggly line that crosses the I-beam three-quarters of the way down the cursor:

2. To reposition the type along the path, select the Path Selection tool, or the Direct Selection tool. Position your cursor at the beginning of the type. When the cursor changes to the I-beam with arrow ( ), click and drag to move the type along the path.

Warp Type

Photoshop provides a variety of preset type warps that you can customize to suit your requirements.

To flip type across a path, select the Selection tool, or the Direct Selection tool. Position your cursor on the type. When the cursor changes to the I-beam with arrow, click and drag the cursor across the path:

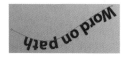

To warp type, make sure that you have selected a type layer in the Layers palette. Click the Warp Type button ( ) in the Options bar. Choose a warp preset effect from the Style pop-up menu. Use the Bend, Horizontal and Vertical Distortion sliders to control the effect. Click OK. Warped type remains editable. Choose None from the Style pop-up menu to remove warping from a type layer.

Paths

An understanding of paths in Photoshop is essential for creating cutouts for use in page layout applications such as QuarkXPress and Adobe InDesign. Paths can also be used to create accurate selections.

You can save paths with the image file in Photoshop format, convert paths into selections, or convert selections into paths. You can also export paths to Adobe Illustrator.

Covers

Chapter Eleven

Converting Selections to Paths

A quick technique for creating a path is to make a selection, convert the selection into a work path, and then into a path.

Use Window> Show Paths to show the Paths palette.

1 First make a selection using any of the selection tools. Then, choose Make Work Path from the Paths palette menu.

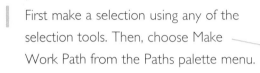

2 The Make Work Path dialog box appears. Specify a Tolerance value (from 0.5–10).

The Tolerance value controls how closely the path conforms to the selection. A low Tolerance value creates a path that follows the selection tightly, but creates a greater number of points. A high Tolerance value produces a path that follows the selection more loosely, but with fewer points.

3 OK the dialog box. A work path appears in the Paths palette, along with a thumbnail of the path. The selection disappears. Choose Save Path from the pop-up menu if you want to save this path before making any adjustments to it. Enter a name. OK the dialog box. The new path appears in the palette, replacing the work path.

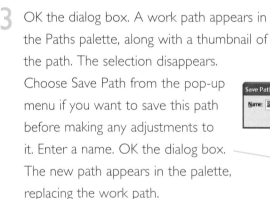

You can only have one work path in the Paths palette at any one time. A work path is a temporary path only. For a path to be saved when you save your file, you must first save the path.

4 To hide the path, click in empty space in the Paths palette. To show the path, click on the path name to select it. The path highlights.

Converting paths to selections

You can also convert a path into a selection. This is useful when you want a very accurate selection.

To convert a path into a selection, click on the path in the Paths palette to highlight it. Then choose Make Selection from the palette menu, or click the Load Path as Selection icon.

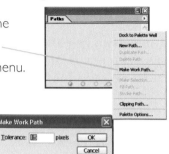

Creating Paths Using the Pen Tool

You can use the Pen tool to create paths. When you start to create a path it appears as a "work path" in the Paths palette. A work path is only a temporary path.

The Pen tool creates anchor points which are connected by straight lines or curved segments. You can use the other tools in the Paths tool group to modify a path by adding, deleting or moving anchor points, and by changing the nature of the point, from smooth to corner and vice versa. You can also edit curved segments by dragging the Bézier direction points.

Use the Paths palette menu to create a new path before you use the Pen tool to automatically save the path without going through the intermediary stage of a work path.

To create a path, select the Pen tool in the Toolbox. Make sure the Create Path icon is selected. You can select the Rubber Band option from the drop down triangle in the Options bar to see a preview of the line segments as you draw.

You can press the Delete key to delete the last anchor point. If you press Delete twice, you will delete the entire path.

Position your cursor where you want to start drawing the path, then click, release the button, move the mouse and click again to create a straight line segment. Continue moving your cursor and clicking to create further straight line segments.

Use the Freeform Pen tool to create a path by clicking and dragging the mouse. This is similar to drawing with a pencil. You have no control over where Photoshop places anchor points, but you can easily edit the path after it is drawn.

Alternatively, you can click and drag to set an anchor point and create direction lines for a curve segment. Then, release the button and move the cursor, and again click and drag to create the next anchor point with direction lines. Continue in this way to create the path you want. Position the Pen tool cursor at the start point. Notice the cursor now has a small circle attached to it. Click to create a closed path. The path will appear in the Paths palette with the default title of Work Path.

You can only have one work path in a file. It is a good idea to save the path and give it a name, so you do not delete it accidentally by creating another work path. See page 144 for details on saving your work path.

4 To create an open path, follow the techniques outlined in steps 1–3 but instead of clicking back at the start point click on the Pen tool in the Toolbox to finish the path. This is now an open path to which you could, for example, apply a stroke.

Creating corner points

As you use the Pen tool to create paths, you can draw corner points as you go, in combination with straight line segments and smooth points. In many instances, a smooth point cannot create the shape of the path you want.

Provided that Auto Add/Delete is selected in the Options bar, you can use the Pen tool to add and delete anchor points. The tool cursor changes intelligently, depending on whether you position the cursor on an anchor point or a line segment.

A corner point allows a sharp change of direction at the anchor point. In a corner point, the direction points can be manipulated independently. This is what makes them essential to create paths that require sharp changes of direction.

1 To draw a corner point, click and drag as you would to set a smooth point. Concentrate on getting the shape of the path coming into the point correct. Release the mouse button.

The paths in these illustrations have been moved one pixel away from the edge of the leaf so that they display more clearly. When you create a clipping path, it is best to position the path a pixel or so inside the shape you want to cut out, to avoid unwanted edge pixels being included. Unwanted edge pixels are sometimes referred to as "edge tear".

2 Position your cursor on the anchor point, hold down Alt/option, then click and drag off the point. This converts the point to a corner point. You are now controlling the direction of the outgoing curve segment. As you drag the second direction point, notice that it no longer has any effect on the incoming direction point.

3 Move your cursor to a new position, then continue drawing either smooth or corner points.

Showing and Selecting Paths/Points

Use the following techniques for selecting, deselecting and deleting paths.

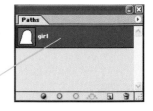

1 To select a path, first you have to show it. To do this, click the path entry in the Paths palette. The path now shows in the image window.

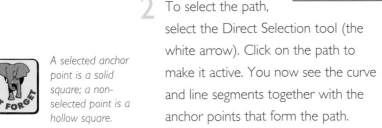

2 To select the path, select the Direct Selection tool (the white arrow). Click on the path to make it active. You now see the curve and line segments together with the anchor points that form the path.

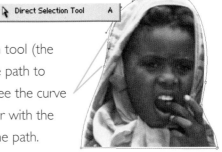

A selected anchor point is a solid square; a non-selected point is a hollow square.

3 Click on the anchor point of a curve segment to select the point and display the direction points.

4 To select and move an entire path, show the path, then hold down Alt/option and click on the path. Using the Direct Selection tool, position your cursor on an anchor point or curve segment, then click and drag to reposition the path. To deselect a path, click away from the path using the Direct Selection tool. The path still shows, but is not selected.

To improve the clarity of these illustrations, the path has been moved one pixel away from the edge of the image.

5 To delete a path, with a point or line segment of the path selected press Delete twice. Alternatively, with the entire path selected, press Delete once. You can also drag the path name onto the Wastebasket icon in the Paths palette.

Add, Delete and Convert Points

To achieve a precise path, you often need to add points and delete points on a path.

For a smooth point, when you drag one of the direction points in a circular direction, the other point balances it to maintain a smooth curve at the anchor point.

A corner point is one which allows a sharp change of direction at the anchor point. Notice that for a corner point, when you drag one of the direction points, the other point is not affected. You have complete, independent control over each direction point.

The Add Anchor Point tool cursor appears as a hollow arrow until you position it on a path. It then becomes the Pen cursor with an additional plus (+) symbol. Similarly, the Delete Anchor Point tool cursor only appears when you position the cursor on an existing anchor point.

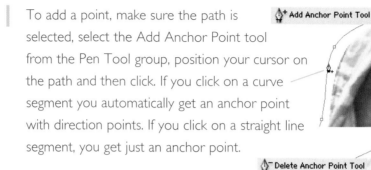

1 To add a point, make sure the path is selected, select the Add Anchor Point tool from the Pen Tool group, position your cursor on the path and then click. If you click on a curve segment you automatically get an anchor point with direction points. If you click on a straight line segment, you get just an anchor point.

2 To delete a point, make sure the path is selected, select the Delete Anchor Point tool, position your cursor on an existing anchor point then click. The path redraws without the point.

3 To convert a smooth point into a corner point, select an anchor point with the Direct Selection tool. Select the Convert Point tool, position your cursor on a direction point then click and drag. Use the Direct Selection tool to make any further changes to the direction points.

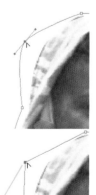

4 To convert anchor points on straight line segments into smooth points, select the Convert Point tool, position your cursor on the anchor point then click and drag. Direction lines appear around the point. Use the Direct Selection tool to make any further changes to the points.

5 To convert a smooth point into a corner point without direction lines, select the Convert Point tool then click on an anchor point.

Editing Points

Paths invariably need to be modified and fine-tuned to produce the result you require.

Select the Direct Selection tool to edit paths and points (see page 147, "Showing and Selecting Paths/Points").

Direct Selection Tool   A

1 To edit a smooth point, make sure the path is selected, then click on the anchor point to select it. Direction points appear either side of the anchor point. Direction points control the shape and length of a curve segment.

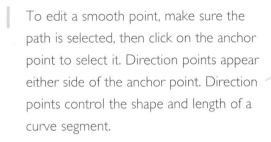

Select an anchor point and press the arrow keys to move the selected point in 1-pixel increments.

2 When you drag a direction point of a smooth anchor point, as you change the angle of one side, the other direction point moves to balance the point you are moving. This ensures the curve is always smooth through the anchor point.

With the Pen tool selected, hold down Command/ Ctrl to toggle temporarily to the Direct Selection tool. Hold down Alt/option to toggle to the Convert Point tool (when the cursor is positioned directly over an anchor point or direction point).

3 The further away from the anchor point you drag a direction point, the longer the associated curve segment becomes. As the curve segment is anchored at the anchor points at either end, this causes the curve segment to bow out more. Bring the direction point closer to the anchor point and the curve segment becomes shorter.

4 When you drag direction points on a corner anchor point, each moves totally independently of the other, allowing a sharp change of direction at the point.

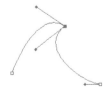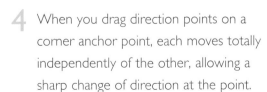

Exporting Paths

Exporting Clipping Paths

Create a clipping path when you want to create transparent areas in an image you intend to use in an application such as QuarkXPress or Adobe InDesign. A clipping path makes areas of the image outside the path transparent, allowing you to see past the outline of the image to the background on which the image is placed.

Flatness allows a PostScript printer to create less memory-intensive paths at output. If you use too high a flatness value, you get an approximate path that does not accurately conform to the path you created.

For high-resolution printing (1200–2400 dpi) a flatness value of 8 to 10 should be acceptable. Use a value of 1 to 3 for low resolution printing (300–600 dpi). Leave the field blank to use the printer's default setting. This usually produces good results with most images.

Remember to convert the file to an appropriate mode – e.g. CMYK – before you save the file in EPS format.

Select a TIFF preview option if you intend to use the image on the Windows platform.

1 Create a saved path (see page 144). If you have more than one path in the Paths palette, make sure you select the appropriate path. Use the Paths palette menu to select Clipping Path.

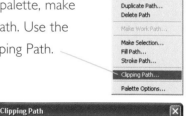

2 Use the Path pop-up to specify a different path to make into a clipping path if necessary. Enter a Flatness value.

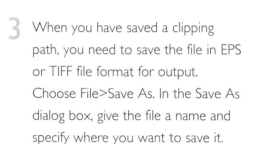

3 When you have saved a clipping path, you need to save the file in EPS or TIFF file format for output. Choose File>Save As. In the Save As dialog box, give the file a name and specify where you want to save it.

4 Choose Photoshop EPS or TIFF from the Format pop-up. Click Save. Clipping Paths saved with the image are automatically exported with the file when you save in Photoshop EPS or TIFF file format.

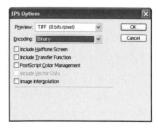

5 See the section on saving in Photoshop EPS format (page 46) for information on Preview and Encoding options.

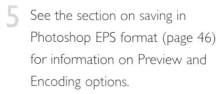

Save a file with a clipping path in Photoshop EPS format if you are printing the file to a PostScript output device.

6 When you import the file into a QuarkXPress or Adobe InDesign page, the clipping path hides areas of the image outside the clipping path. The second version of the same image on this Quark page has a black background and does not have a clipping path.

Exporting paths to Adobe Illustrator

Sometimes it is useful to export a path from Photoshop into Adobe Illustrator to perform further manipulation on it.

1 To export a path to Adobe Illustrator, choose File>Export> Paths to Illustrator. In the Export Paths dialog box, change the name if necessary but leave the automatically generated .ai extension to distinguish the file. If your Photoshop document has more than one saved path, use the Paths pop-up to choose the path you want to export. Click Save.

When you open exported paths in Adobe Illustrator, the crop marks indicate the dimensions of the original Photoshop image.

You can use the Export Paths to Illustrator command and then open the file in Macromedia FreeHand if you do not have Adobe Illustrator.

2 Use File>Open in Adobe Illustrator to import the path. Manipulate and make changes to the path as required, then save the Illustrator file in EPS format.

3 See page 40 for information on placing an Illustrator EPS into Photoshop.

Creating Shape Layers

The Shape tools allow you to create lines, rectangles, ovals and circles. In Photoshop you can also create polygons and custom shapes. Use the Options bar to set specific options for each tool individually.

1. To draw a rectangle as a Shape layer, first choose a foreground color for the shape. Select the Rectangle tool. Make sure the Shape Layer button is selected in the Options bar.

2. Position your cursor in the image window. Drag diagonally to define the size of the shape. A new Shape layer appears in the Layers palette. To create additional shapes on the same Shape layer, either choose a new shape tool from the Options bar or use the same tool. Select the Add to Shape Area button in the Options bar. Draw the shape.

3. To draw a square, hold down Shift then drag with the Rectangle tool. Release the mouse button before you release Shift, otherwise the constraint effect will be lost. Hold down Alt/option then drag with the Rectangle tool to draw a rectangle from the center out.

4. Select the Shape layer icon (a highlight border appears around the Shape layer icon), then use the Direct Selection tool to select and then make changes to the shape of the object in the image window on the Shape layer.

Channels and Masks

The Channels palette stores color information about an image and can also be used to store selections on a permanent basis.

Masks are created and used in a variety of ways in Photoshop. The basic principle of masks is that you use them to protect areas of an image from editing that you carry out on the unmasked areas of the image.

Use Quick Mask mode when you don't want to save the mask for future use. Layer masks control how different areas of pixels on a layer are hidden or revealed.

Covers

Chapter Twelve

Quick Mask Mode

In Quick Mask mode you create a 50% red, semi-transparent overlay. This overlay represents the protected area of the image. The overlay is similar in concept to a traditional rubylith mask. Quick Mask mode is particularly useful because you can see both the image and the mask as you create and fine-tune the mask.

You can make a rough selection first, then go into Quick Mask mode and edit the mask further if necessary.

1 To create a quick mask, click the Quick Mask Mode icon in the Toolbox. Make sure that the default foreground and background colors are black and white respectively.

2 Show the Brushes palette and choose a brush size. Use a hard-edged brush to create selections with a clearly defined edge. Use a soft-edged brush to create selections that are slightly softer along the edge. Select a painting tool and drag across your image to "paint" in the mask. Painting with black adds to the mask. Although you see through the 50% red mask, the pixels covered by the mask are completely protected.

Painting with gray or any other color creates a semi-transparent or partial mask.

3 To remove areas from the mask you can use the Eraser tool, or paint with white.

4 When you are satisfied with your mask, click the Standard Mode button. This turns the areas of the image that were not part of your quick mask into a selection. You can now make changes to the selected areas (in this example the Smart Blur filter has been applied), leaving the areas that were the quick mask unchanged.

The Channels Palette

The Channels palette (Window>Channels) shows a breakdown of the color components that combine to make up the composite color image that you work with most of the time on-screen.

You can change the display of channels from grayscale to the color they represent by choosing Edit>Preferences>Display and Cursor. Select Color Channels in Color.

For example, in RGB mode, there are four channels – the composite image (all the other channels combined), and then a channel each for the red, green and blue color components of the image. In CMYK mode, there are five channels.

Using the Channels palette you can be selective about which of the color components in your image you change.

1   To switch to a specific channel, click the channel name in the Channels palette. The channel highlights to indicate that it is selected. The image window changes according to the channel you chose.

Indexed Color mode, Grayscale mode and Bitmap mode all have only one channel.

2   You can view additional channels by clicking the Eye icon for a channel. The image window changes, but your editing remains limited to the selected channel.

3   Click on the composite channel to return to normal image-editing view.

Saving and Loading Selections

Because you can only have one "active" selection in an image at any one time, the facility to store a selection which can be reloaded later is vital, especially if the selection is complex and took some time to create. You save selections as an extra channel in the Channels palette. These extra channels are referred to as "alpha channels".

Saving selections

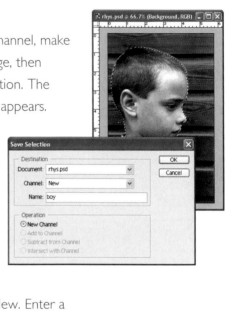

1   To save a selection to a channel, make your selection on the image, then choose Select>Save Selection. The Save Selection dialog box appears. Specify in which document you wish to save the channel. (You can save channels in another document to keep the file size of the current document as small as possible.) Leave the Channel pop-up on New. Enter a name for the channel. Click OK. Alternatively, make your selection and then click the Save Selection icon in the Channels palette.

2   In the Channels palette, you will see an extra channel. This is the new "alpha channel". An alpha channel is a grayscale channel.

3   When you have saved a selection to an alpha channel you can freely deselect the selection in your image, as you can now reselect exactly the same area at any time using the alpha channel.

Loading selections

Use the following process to reselect an area using the alpha channel:

File formats that can retain alpha channel information when you save include: Photoshop, PDF, PICT and TIFF.

1   To load a channel selection as a selection on the image, make sure the composite image is displayed. You can do this by clicking on the topmost channel name in the Channels palette. Then choose Select>Load Selection. The Load Selection dialog box appears.

2   Use the Channel pop-up menu to specify which channel you want to load. Select an operation as appropriate. The operations allow you to control how the selection you are about to load interacts with any existing selection in the image – adding to it, subtracting from it or intersecting with it. Click OK.

When you are working in Quick Mask mode, you can turn the quick mask into an alpha channel by dragging the quick mask entry that appears in the Channels palette onto the New Channel icon:

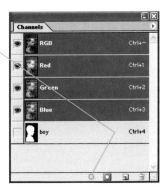

3   Alternatively, using the Channels palette, drag the channel you want to load onto the Load Selection icon.

4   To delete a channel, drag the channel name onto the Wastebasket icon at the bottom of the palette.

Editing Alpha Channel Masks

You can display an alpha channel without loading it onto the image as a selection. You can then edit the mask by painting with black, white or gray.

1 To display an alpha channel, choose Windows>Channels to display the Channels palette. Click on the alpha channel you want to display. The channel name, and an Eye icon in the left column of the palette, indicate that this is the visible channel.

2 The image window changes from the composite view to a grayscale representation of the mask. The white area represents the selection and the black portions represent the protected areas.

If you paint with gray you can create a semi-transparent mask.

3 To edit a selection channel, select a painting tool and brush size. Click the Default Colors icon if necessary, to change the foreground color to black. Paint with black to remove areas from the selection. Paint with white on any black portion of the mask to add it to the selection.

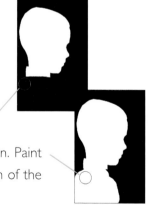

Make sure you do not have a selection showing (marching ants) before you attempt to modify or edit the selection mask channel.

Another useful technique for editing a selection mask is to view a mask and image simultaneously by turning the alpha channel selection into a colored mask (very much like using Quick Mask mode) and then reshaping the mask by painting with black, white or shades of gray.

Reshaping masks

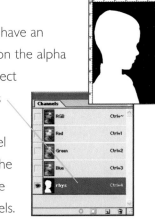

1 To reshape a mask, ensure you don't have an active selection on your image. Click on the alpha channel in the Channels palette to select it. It highlights and the Eye icon shows on the left. The image window now displays the grayscale selection channel mask. The Eye icon disappears from the Composite RGB channel and from the individual Red, Green and Blue channels.

Typically, when you edit masks, you will paint with black or white, with the Mode set to Normal and an Opacity of 100%. However, you can reduce the opacity or pressure settings in order to create a partial mask.

2 Click in the currently empty Eye icon position for the Composite channel. The eye appears for the Composite channel and in the individual Red, Green and Blue ones. The Composite channel now also shows in the image window but only the alpha channel is selected – indicated by the highlight.

3 The image window changes in appearance. The selection area appears as normal whilst the protected or masked portions of the image have a quick mask type transparent film applied.

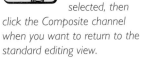

Make sure that the Eye icon for an alpha channel mask is not selected, then click the Composite channel when you want to return to the standard editing view.

4 Select the Brush or Pencil tool. Paint with white to remove areas of the image from the mask (to enlarge the unmasked area). Paint with black to add portions of the image to the mask.

Layer Masks

Use layer masks to hide or reveal areas of a layer. A layer mask is extremely useful because you can use it to try out effects without actually changing the pixels on the layer. When you have achieved the result you want, you can apply the mask as a permanent change. If you are not satisfied, you can discard the mask without having permanently affected the pixels on the layer.

For information on creating layers, see Chapter Nine. For information on using filters, see Chapter Fourteen.

This example begins with an image with two layers. The Background layer is the original scan; the other layer was created using the Render>Clouds filter.

1 To create a layer mask for the Clouds layer, first click on the layer to make it active. Choose Layer>Add Layer Mask>Reveal All. Reveal All means that all the pixels in the layer are visible. The Clouds layer now completely obscures the Background layer.

You can have only one layer mask per layer.

2 In the Layers palette, the layer mask is active, indicated by the Mask icon next to the Eye icon. Click on the layer thumbnail to make the layer active (the Paintbrush icon indicates that you can now work directly on the layer). Click on the Layer Mask thumbnail to continue editing the mask.

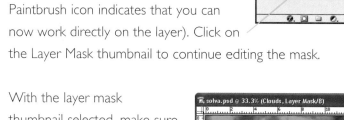

3 With the layer mask thumbnail selected, make sure that the foreground color is set to black. Choose a Painting tool and start painting. Painting with black hides pixels on the Clouds layer, revealing pixels on the Background layer.

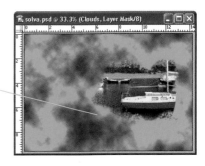

4 Pixels on the Clouds layer are not permanently erased when you paint with black. Paint with white to show pixels on the Clouds layer – in effect hiding pixels on the Background layer. (If you choose Layer>Add Layer Mask>Hide All, you start with the opposite scenario to the above. Now all the pixels on the Clouds layer are hidden. Paint with white to reveal pixels on the Clouds layer, paint with black to hide them.)

You can paint with shades of gray to partially hide pixels on the Clouds layer.

5 To temporarily switch off the layer mask, choose Layer>Disable Mask, or hold down Shift then click on the Layer Mask icon. To reactivate the mask, choose Layer>Enable Layer Mask, or hold down Shift then click again on the Layer Mask icon.

6 To apply the layer mask as a permanent change, choose Layer>Remove Layer Mask>Apply. To discard the layer mask, without affecting pixels on the layer, choose Layer>Remove Layer Mask>Discard.

7 Or drag the Layer Mask icon (not the Layer icon) onto the Wastebasket icon in the bottom of the palette. Click Apply or Discard. Once you apply a layer mask you lose the flexibility of making further changes – the effect is fixed. Click Discard only if you want to delete the mask.

Channel and Quick Mask Options

The Channel Options dialog box and the Quick Mask Options dialog box allow you to control the color of a mask and whether the protected or unprotected area of the image is colored with the overlay.

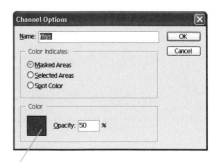

1 To change channel options, double-click the alpha channel entry. Alternatively, with the alpha channel selected, use the Channels palette menu to choose Channel Options.

2 In the Channel Options dialog box you can enter a new name for the channel. You can also choose Selected Areas to reverse the way in which the color will apply. In other words, masked (protected) areas will appear white, while the selection area (unprotected) will appear black.

3 To change the color used to represent the masked (protected) area and its opacity, click the Color box and choose a new color from the Color Picker.

4 To change the settings for a quick mask, double-click either the Quick Mask Mode icon or the Standard Mode icon, then make the appropriate changes in the dialog box that appears.

Color Correction Techniques

Color correction involves making changes to the overall brightness and contrast in an image and also the color balance to compensate for any tonal deficiencies and color casts in the original image.

You should bear in mind that although color corrections can improve the overall appearance of an image, inevitably some color values may be lost – certain pixels in the original scan that were different colors can end up remapped to the same color. The successful use of the commands covered in this chapter can also depend on the accuracy of the colors you see on your monitor.

Covers

Chapter Thirteen

Brightness/Contrast and Color Balance

The Brightness/Contrast command provides the least complicated controls for changing overall brightness/contrast levels in an image. It does not change individual color channels; it makes the same adjustment to all pixels across the full tonal range of the image.

Click the Preview button in the Brightness/Contrast dialog box to see, on-screen, the result of the settings you choose as you make the changes.

To change brightness and contrast for an entire image, or for a selection, choose Image>Adjustments> Brightness/Contrast. Drag the Brightness and Contrast sliders or enter a value in the entry boxes. OK the dialog box.

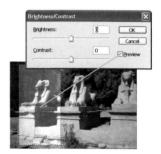

The Color Balance dialog box provides general controls for correcting an overall color cast in an image. As such, it provides the least complex method of color correction.

Choose Image>Adjustments>Auto Contrast to automatically adjust the contrast for an image or selection. Auto Contrast does not adjust individual channels in an image. It makes highlights appear lighter and shadows darker by mapping the lightest and darkest pixels in the image to white and black respectively.

Color Balance works on the principle of complementary colors. If there is too much cyan in an image, you drag the Cyan–Red slider towards red to remove the cyan color cast; for too much magenta, drag the Magenta–Green slider towards green etc.

Work on the composite view of an image when using the Color Balance dialog box.

To adjust the Color Balance of an image, choose Image> Adjust>Color Balance. Click the Shadows, Midtones or Highlights radio button to specify the tonal range to which you want to make changes. Drag the color sliders to reduce/increase the amount of a color in the image. Select Preserve Luminosity to prevent brightness values from changing as you change color levels. This helps maintain the overall color balance in the image.

You should use the Color Balance dialog box with caution, and only if your monitor is calibrated accurately, as you need to be certain that the color adjustments you see on screen accurately represent colors at final output.

Auto Levels and Auto Color

You can also use the Auto Levels command from within the Levels and Curves dialog boxes. Click the Auto button:

Auto Levels allows you to adjust brightness and contrast automatically. Auto Levels examines each color channel independently and changes the darkest pixels to black and the lightest pixels to white, then redistributes the remaining shades of gray between these two points.

Auto Levels works best on images that have a reasonably even distribution of tonal values throughout the image, as it redistributes pixels based on white and black points, with a tendency to increase contrast.

Auto Color removes unwanted color casts in an image without adjusting the contrast in an image.

1   To apply Auto Levels to an image, choose Image>Adjustments> Auto Levels. (Use Edit>Undo if you do not like the result.)

2   To apply Auto Color to an image, choose Image>Adjustments> Auto Color. (Use Edit>Undo if you do not like the result.)

Auto Levels adjusts each color channel in the image individually. As a result, it may remove or introduce color casts.

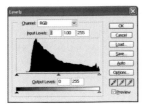

Original   Auto Levels   Auto Color

Both Auto Levels and Auto Color generally produce good results, but they do not allow the precision of manual adjustments that you can make using the Levels and Curves dialog boxes.

The Levels Dialog Box

Use the Levels dialog box (Image>Adjustments>Levels) to adjust the tonal balance for color and grayscale images. You can adjust highlight, shadow and midtone ranges for a selection or an entire image, or you can make changes to individual channels only.

Input Levels

The Input Levels sliders and entry boxes allow you to improve the contrast in a "flat" image.

The most flexible way of working with Levels, Curves and Color Balance is to set up Adjustment layers (see page 121). Adjustment layers allow you to readjust settings in the respective dialog boxes until you are satisfied with the result.

1 Use the Channel pop-up menu to select a channel. If you do not select an individual channel, you can work on the composite image and affect all channels.

2 To darken an image, drag the solid black slider to the right. Alternatively, enter an appropriate value in the leftmost Input Levels entry box.

The spiky graph in the middle of the Levels dialog box is a Histogram. See pages 170–171 for an explanation of the Histogram in the Levels dialog box.

This maps or clips pixels to black. For example, if you drag the black slider to 15, all pixels with an original value between 0 and 15 become black. The result is a darker image.

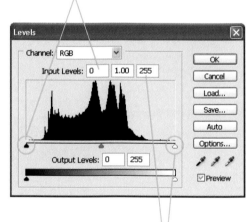

Dragging either or both the black or white Input Levels sliders inwards has the effect of increasing contrast in the image.

3 To lighten an image, drag the hollow, white Input Levels slider to the left. Alternatively, enter an appropriate value in the rightmost Input Levels entry box. The result is to map or clip pixels to white. For example, if you drag the white slider to 245, all pixels with an original value between 245 and 255 become white. The result is a lighter image.

Gamma

The gray triangle and the middle Input Levels entry box control the Gamma value in the image. The Gamma value is the brightness level of mid-gray pixels in the image.

When you OK the Levels dialog box, you can use Edit>Undo/Redo a number of times to evaluate the changes.

1 To lighten midtones, drag the gray slider to the left, or increase the Gamma value in the Input Levels entry box above the default setting of 1.00.

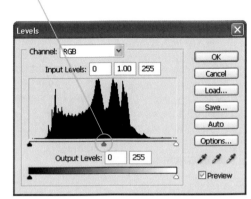

2 To darken midtones, drag the gray slider to the right, or decrease the Gamma value in the Input Levels entry box.

Output Levels

You can use the Output Levels entry boxes or sliders to decrease the amount of contrast in an image.

See page 165 for an explanation of Auto Levels and the Auto button.

1 Drag the black Output Levels slider to the right to lighten the image and reduce the contrast.

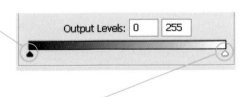

2 Drag the white Output Levels slider to the left to darken the image and reduce the contrast.

The Curves Dialog Box

The Curves dialog box (Image>Adjustments>Curves) offers the most versatile set of controls for making tonal adjustments in an image. The central Brightness graph in the dialog box displays the original and adjusted brightness values for pixels in the image. The graph is a straight line from 0 (black) to 255 (white), before any adjustments are made – input and output values for pixels are the same.

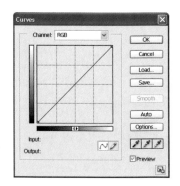

You should be careful not to click on the Brightness bar at the bottom of the Curves dialog box accidentally. The default Brightness bar

starts black and graduates to white. In this state, the brightness curve indicates the brightness values of colors in the image; the brightness curve starts at 0, for black, and moves to 255, for white.

The horizontal axis of the graph represents the original or input values, the vertical axis represents the output or adjusted values. By adjusting the brightness curve, you are remapping the brightness values of pixels in the image.

1. To add a point to the curve, select the Point tool. Click on the curve. (You can add up to fifteen points.) Drag the point(s) around to edit the curve. Or click at a point in the graph and the curve will change according to where you clicked.

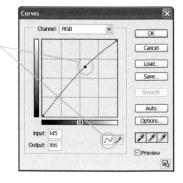

2. To delete a point, click on a point to select it, then press the Delete/Backspace key. You can also drag it outside the Brightness graph.

Select a point on the graph, then press the arrow keys on your keyboard to move the point in increments.

3. To lighten an image, select the Point tool, position your cursor near the midpoint of the graph, then click to place a new point. Click and drag this point upwards.

...cont'd

*Hold down Alt/
option, then click
on the Reset
button (previously
Cancel) to restore
the original settings in the
dialog box.*

4 To darken an image, select the
Point tool, position your cursor
near the midpoint of the graph,
then click to place a point.
Drag the point downwards.

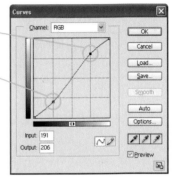

5 To increase the contrast in an
image, place a point at roughly the
¼ tone part of the graph and drag
this upwards to lighten the
highlights. Next, place a point at
roughly the ¾ tone part of the
graph. Drag this downward to
darken the shadow areas. The
result is to increase the contrast in
the image by lightening the
highlights and darkening the
shadows, whilst leaving the midtones more or less untouched.

6 Reverse the setting in step 5 to decrease the contrast in an image.

7 To limit changes to the midtones and highlights, click on the
graph to place a point at the ¾ tone. Place a point at the

¼ tone and drag
this upwards.
Reverse this procedure
to change midtones
and shadows without
affecting highlights.

The Histogram Palette

A histogram is a bar chart that represents the distribution of pixels in an image. Shadows are on the left side of the histogram, highlights on the right and midtones in the middle. The spread of pixels through the shadows, midtones and highlights represents the tonal balance in an image.

Having the Histogram palette visible as you work on an image can help you evaluate the effect of the changes and adjustments you make.

In a histogram, the horizontal axis plots color or luminosity levels from 0–255. The vertical axis plots the number of pixels at each level.

1 The Histogram palette is grouped initially with the Navigator and Info palettes. Click the Histogram tab, or choose Window>Histogram to show the palette.

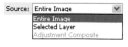

2 Choose Expand View from the Histogram palette menu to enable access to the Channel drop down menu. Choose from RGB, Luminosity, and Colors to view the histogram for the channel you specify. For an image with more than one layer you can choose Selected Layer from the Source drop down menu to view a histogram for the pixel content on the currently active layer.

When in All Channels view, choosing an option from the Channels drop down menu changes the top histogram only.

3 Choose All Channels View to display an extended palette with histograms for all channels in the image, with the exception of Alpha channels, Spot channels and masks. The topmost histogram represents the luminance, or overall brightness values for the composite channel.

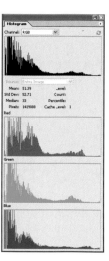

4 For RGB and CMYK images you can choose Colors from the Channel drop down menu to display a composite histogram of the individual color channels in color.

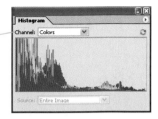

5 To show statistical information for the histogram, choose Show Statistics from the Histogram palette menu. Move your cursor through the bars of the histogram itself to get readouts for Level, Count and Percentile in the statistics area.

6 When working in dialog boxes such as Levels and Curves, provided that the Preview option is selected, the Histogram palette updates as you make changes to the settings in the dialog box.

7 The Cached Data warning icon appears when the Histogram palette display is based on information held in cache (an area of short term memory) rather than the actual current state of the image. To ensure that the histogram represents all pixels in the image in their current state, either click the Cached Data warning icon, or click the Uncached Refresh button. You can also double-click anywhere within the histogram. Photoshop uses cached information for the image in order to display information in the histogram quickly, but slightly less accurately, as the cached information is based on a representative sampling of pixels in the image only.

Shadow/Highlight Command

The Shadow/Highlight command is useful for images with strong backlighting resulting in a silhouette effect on the foreground elements. The default settings in the Shadow/Highlight dialog box are intended to improve images with backlighting problems. You can also use the Shadow/Highlight command to lighten shadows.

1 To adjust shadows and highlights in an image, choose Image>Adjustments>Shadow/Highlight.

2 Drag the Shadows Amount slider to the right, or enter a value in the percentage entry field from 0 – 100 to lighten the shadows. The higher the value the greater the degree of lightening.

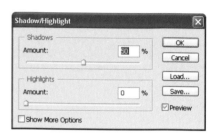

3 Drag the Highlights Amount slider to the right to darken the highlights. You can also enter a value in the percentage entry field. The higher the value the greater the degree of darkening.

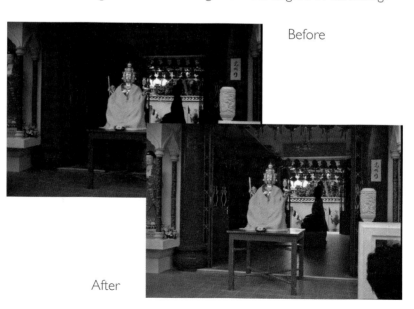

Before

After

Match Color Command

Use the Match Color command when you need to make colors in one image (the destination image), consistent with colors in another image (the source image). You can also use this command to match colors between layers within the same image.

To match colors in an image to colors in a different image, select the destination image. Choose Image>Adjustments>Match Color. If the destination image has multiple layers, make sure you select the layer you want to match before you choose the Match Colors command.

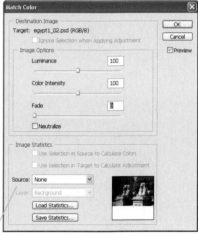

2. In the Image Statistics area of the dialog box, use the Source drop down menu to select the source image which contains the color characteristics you want to match. If necessary, use the Layer drop down menu to select a specific layer within the source image, or leave the option set to Merged to use the overall color statistics of the source image.

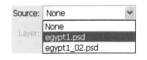

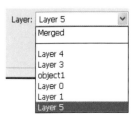

3 In the Image Options area of the dialog box, drag the Fade slider to reduce the intensity of the color adjustment in the target image if necessary. Drag the Luminance slider to increase or decrease the brightness of

the result. Drag the Color Intensity slider to increase or decrease the overall color saturation.

Matching colors between layers

1 To match color characteristics from one layer to another in the same image, make sure you have the destination layer (the layer whose color you want to change) selected.

2 Choose Image>Adjustments>Match Color. In the Image Statistics area set the Source drop down menu to the name of the file with which you are working.

3 From the Layer drop down menu select a specific layer, or choose Merged to match color characteristics from the whole of the image.

4 Use the Fade, Luminance and Color Intensity sliders to fine tune the results.

Filters

Photoshop ships with more than 95 filters as standard. Filters add enormous creative flexibility and potential to image-manipulation, and they are well worth experimenting with.

You can use filters across an entire image, or you can apply them to selections to limit the results to specific areas. Filters cannot be applied to images in Bitmap or Indexed Color mode. Some filters are not available in CMYK mode.

Covers

Chapter Fourteen

Filter Controls

Use the Filter menu to access the Photoshop filters. Many of the filters have standard controls, which are explained below:

If you have the Preview box checked, click and hold on the Preview window inside the filter's dialog box to see the image without the filter settings applied.

Choose Edit>Fade Filter to reduce the effect of a filter on an image.

Use Command+F (Mac) or Ctrl+F (Windows) to reapply the last-used filter and settings.

A line flashing under the Preview check box means that Photoshop is still rendering the new settings.

2 Click and drag on the image in the Preview window to scroll around to preview different parts of the image. Alternatively, with the filter's dialog box active, position your cursor in the main image window – the cursor becomes a hollow box – then click to set the view in the Preview window.

1 Click the Preview check box to see the effect of your settings previewed in the main image window, as well as in the Preview window inside the filter dialog box.

3 Click the "+" or "–" buttons to zoom in or out on areas of the image. You can also use the Command+ Spacebar (Mac) or Ctrl+Spacebar (Windows) keyboard shortcuts within the Preview window or the image window.

4 Hold down Alt/option and click the Reset button (previously Cancel) to revert to the original settings in the dialog box.

5 After you OK a filter's dialog box, use Command+F (Mac) or Ctrl+F (Windows) to reapply the last-used filter and its settings.

Unsharp Mask and Sharpen Filters

These filters allow you to enhance detail in your images.

Unsharp Mask

This is a powerful function which can help you to sharpen blurry images in specific areas. For example, if you rotate an image, or change the dimensions or resolution of the image, it may blur due to any interpolation that Photoshop applies. This can also happen when you convert from RGB to CMYK. Where the Unsharp Mask filter finds edges (areas where there is a high degree of contrast), it increases the contrast between adjacent pixels. The result is to create an apparent improvement in the focus of the image.

It is well worth making a copy of your image to work on before you start experimenting with filters.

1 To use Unsharp Mask to sharpen an image, choose Filter> Sharpen>Unsharp Mask. The Unsharp Mask dialog box appears.

2 Adjust settings for Amount, Radius and Threshold. Click OK or press Return/Enter.

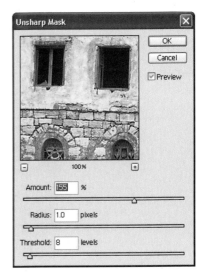

Amount – Use this to control the amount of sharpening applied to the edges (minimum = 1, maximum = 500). The picture will become pixelated if the amount is too high.

Values below 50% produce subtle results; values between 50% and 250% produce moderate results; while values between 300% and 500% produce dramatic, exaggerated results.

The settings for Radius and Threshold need to be taken into account when setting the Amount value (see the next page).

Radius – Radius controls the depth of pixels along the high-contrast edges that are changed.

A low radius value restricts the impact of the filter; higher values distribute the impact. Radius values of 2.0 or lower usually produce acceptable sharpening.

Threshold – Sets a level for the minimum amount of contrast between pixels an area must have before it will be modified. The Threshold value is the difference between two adjacent pixels – as measured in brightness levels – that must occur for Photoshop to recognize them as an edge.

On high-resolution images, use a Threshold value of 8 or higher to apply the sharpening effect to specific areas only.

High Threshold values limit changes to areas where there is a high degree of color difference. Use low values to apply the filter more generally throughout the image.

Sharpen and Sharpen More

Use the Sharpen and Sharpen More filters when an image becomes blurred after resampling. Both filters work by increasing contrast between adjacent pixels throughout the image or selection. Sharpen More has a more pronounced effect than Sharpen.

Sharpen Edges

This filter has a more specific effect, applying sharpening along high-contrast edges. In effect, it has a less global impact on a selection or image than Sharpen and Sharpen More.

Sharpen   Sharpen Edges   Sharpen More   Unsharp Mask

Blur Filters

Blur More produces an effect roughly 3 times stronger than the Blur filter.

The Blur filters reduce the contrast between adjacent pixels along edges where considerable color shifts occur, to create a softening, defocusing effect. Blurring produces the opposite effect to sharpening – which increases the contrast between adjacent pixels.

"Blur" and "Blur More" blur a selection in preset amounts offering only a limited degree of control. For greater control when blurring you can use the Gaussian Blur option, which blurs according to a bell-shaped Gaussian distribution curve.

To Blur a Layer or Selection

Create a selection if you want to limit the effect of the Blur filter to a specific area of your image. Choose Filter>Blur>Blur, or Filter> Blur>Blur More.

Motion Blur

You can use Motion Blur to create the effect of a moving subject or camera.

Angle = 0,
Distance = 12

Angle = -45,
Distance = 12

Angle = -53,
Distance = 26

To create a motion blur, make a selection, if required. Choose Filter>Blur> Motion Blur.

2 Enter a value in the Angle box, or drag the Angle indicator to specify the angle or direction of the blur. Enter a value in the Distance entry box to specify the distance in pixels for the blur effect. OK the dialog box.

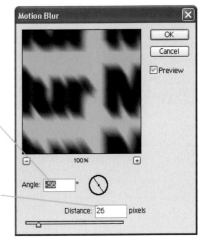

Radial Blur

Radial Blur creates the effect of zooming in as you take a picture.

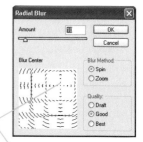

To create a radial blur, make a selection if required. Choose Filter>Blur> Radial Blur.

If you are working on a layer, make sure the Transparency lock is deselected if you want the blur to take effect along the edges of the layer's pixels. (See page 123.)

Select a Blur Method and Quality, and specify an Amount (0–100). Click and drag in the Blur Center window to specify the center point for the zoom or spin effect. OK the dialog box.

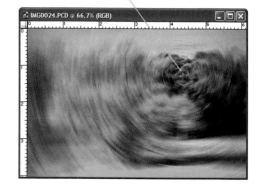

Amount – This value determines the distance pixels are moved to create the blur effect. Higher values produce more intense effects.

Zoom – Zoom creates a zoom-like blurring effect.

Spin – Spin rotates and blurs pixels around a central point.

Quality – Good and Best produce better, smoother results due to the interpolation methods used, but take longer.

Gaussian Blur

Use Gaussian Blur to control the degree of blurring. Gaussian Blur adds low frequency detail to the image or selection. Choose Filter>Blur>Gaussian. Use the Radius slider to adjust the amount of blurring.

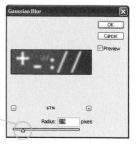

Noise Filters

Add Noise filter

The Add Noise filter randomly distributes high-contrast pixels in an image, creating a grainy effect.

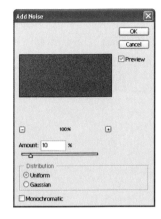

> To add noise, create a selection, or work on the entire image. Choose Filter>Noise>Add Noise. Specify Amount, Distribution and Monochromatic options.

Amount – Determines the degree to which pixels are changed from their original color. Enter a number from 1–999.

You can use Add Noise to reduce banding in graduated fills.

Uniform – Produces an even spread of pixels.

Gaussian – Produces a more dramatic result.

Monochromatic – Choose Monochromatic to distribute grayscale dots.

Add Noise is a good way to begin creating textured backgrounds.

Original, flat background

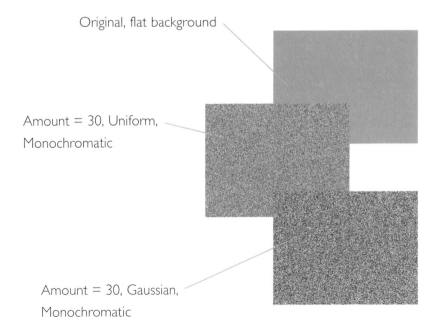

Amount = 30, Uniform, Monochromatic

Amount = 30, Gaussian, Monochromatic

Dust & Scratches filter

Use the Dust & Scratches filter to remove small imperfections and blemishes in a scan caused by dust and scratches. The degree of success you have with this filter depends largely on the image or selection you apply it to.

Radius and Threshold settings are interdependent, and both are taken into account before changes are made.

To remove dust and scratches, create a selection or work on the entire image. Choose Filters> Noise>Dust & Scratches. Specify Radius and Threshold settings. Click OK.

Radius – Determines how small a blemish must be for it to be worked upon by the filter. For example, at a radius of 3 pixels, the Dust & Scratches filter will not attempt to make changes to imperfections above this size.

Threshold – Specifies the minimum amount of contrast between pixels there must be before changes are made.

Despeckle filter

This produces the opposite effect to the Add Noise filter, smoothing and blurring the image, but having little effect on edges.

Median filter

The Median filter also removes noise from a poor-quality scan. It works by averaging the color of adjacent pixels in an image.

To use the Median filter, create a selection, or work on the entire image. Choose Filter>Noise>Median. Specify a Radius value (1–100). OK the dialog box.

The Extract Command

Use the Extract command to isolate an object from its background; especially useful when the object has edges that are not clearly or distinctly defined, such as hair. Make sure you are working on a layer to use the Extract command. If you perform the Extract command on the Background layer it becomes Layer 0 when you OK the dialog box.

1 To extract an object from its background, choose Image>Extract.

2 Select the Edge Highlighter tool (B). In the Tool Options area, set a brush size and choose a color for the edge highlight from the Highlight pop-up.

3 Zoom in on the image if necessary, then draw around the object you want to extract to define the edge. It is important to create a highlight that slightly overlaps both the edge of the foreground object and its background. Use a larger brush size to completely cover more delicate, intricate, "wispy" areas of the foreground object, such as hair; use a smaller brush size to highlight sharper, more defined edges.

4 Use the Eraser tool to undo any mistakes you make with the Edge Highlighter tool. You cannot use the Undo command within the Extract dialog box.

...cont'd

To use an alpha channel as the basis for a selection, choose the alpha channel from the Channel pop-up menu.

Use the Zoom and Hand tools as you would in the Photoshop image window. (See page 24 for further information).

When you have filled an interior area with the Fill tool, clicking again in the fill area clears the fill.

Use the Smooth control in the Extraction area, if necessary, to improve the result of the extraction. The Smooth control can help remove stray artifacts from the extraction by feathering edges slightly:

5   Make sure you completely enclose the object if it has a well-defined interior. It is not necessary to highlight edges where the object touches the edge of the image window.

6   Select the Fill tool (G). Click inside the highlight edge. The interior fills with the Fill color set in the Tool Options area of the dialog.

7   Click the Preview button to preview the results. Use the Display pop-up in the Preview area to set the background against which you see the extracted object. It can help to preview against more than one background color to pick up on any problem areas, before you click OK. (See page 185 for techniques to refine the extraction area.)

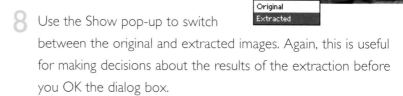

8   Use the Show pop-up to switch between the original and extracted images. Again, this is useful for making decisions about the results of the extraction before you OK the dialog box.

9   OK the dialog box to complete the extraction.

Fine-Tuning Extractions

After you preview the results of the extraction, you will need to fine-tune it, before you OK the dialog box.

1   To make adjustments to the extraction, select the Show Highlight option in the Preview area. The original highlight edge reappears. Click the Hide Fill option to hide the original fill area for the extraction. Choose Original from the View pop-up. The solid background against which you preview the results of the extraction disappears and the original background pixels reappear.

2   Use the Eraser tool to erase parts of the highlight edge and use the Edge Highlighter tool to redefine areas of the edge, as necessary.

3   When you have finished editing the highlight edge, select the Fill tool, then click inside the edge to recreate the fill area. Click the Preview button to preview your changes. Repeat the editing process as necessary until you are satisfied with the result, then click OK.

4   If there are still problems with the extraction, switch off the edge highlight. Use the Clean Up tool to remove any unwanted pixels around the extraction after you preview it. Hold down Alt/option, then drag with the Clean Up tool to refill any unwanted gaps in the extracted object.

5   Use the Edge Touch Up tool to create a more clearly defined, sharper edge in areas where there are problems with the extraction. Click OK to finish the extraction.

The Liquify Dialog Box

The Liquify dialog box allows you to create a wide variety of distortions for retouching images or for achieving creative effects. The dialog box has tools that can push, pull, rotate, reflect, pucker and bloat areas of the image.

Use the Zoom and Hand tools as you would in the standard Photoshop image window.

You must rasterize a Type layer or a Shape layer before you can use the Liquify command.

Only the active layer is distorted by the Liquify dialog box.

Hold down Alt/ option then click the Restore All button to revert to the original state of the image.

1. To distort an entire layer, select the layer, or make a selection on a layer to define an area for distortion. Choose Filter>Liquify.

2. Freeze areas of the image that you don't want to change using the Freeze Mask tool. Set a Brush size, then drag across areas of the image you want to freeze. Frozen areas appear as a semi-transparent, red mask. Use the Thaw Mask tool to make frozen areas editable again.

3. Set tool options. Choose a brush size from the Brush Size slider. Set a brush pressure. Lower pressure settings distort the image more slowly allowing you more control over the distortion. Brush Density controls the softness of the edge of the brush. Choose Turbulent Jitter settings to control how tightly the Turbulence tool distorts pixels.

4. Select a tool with which to distort the image. (See the facing page for information on the tools.) Drag in the image to create the distortion. You can press the left mouse button without dragging the mouse to create effects with tools such as the Twirl tools. Set a Brush Rate to control the speed at which distortions happen when you keep the mouse still. Click OK to accept the changes.

Liquify Distortion Tools

There are 7 distortion tools to choose from. Remember to create tool settings for Brush size, Pressure and Turbulent Jitter before you use the tools. Distortions are most pronounced at the center of the brush area. You can create distortions by dragging across pixels, or simply by holding down the left mouse button.

1 Use the Forward Warp tool to distort pixels in a forward direction as you drag.

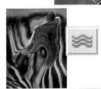

2 Use the Turbulence tool to smoothly mix or scramble pixels. This can sometimes create interesting cloud and wavelike effects.

3 Use the Twirl Clockwise tool to rotate pixels around the brush area in a clockwise direction. Hold down Alt/option to twirl in a counter clockwise direction.

4 Use the Pucker tool to concentrate pixel detail into the center of the brush area.

5 Use the Bloat tool to disperse image detail away from the center of the brush.

Use the Reconstruct tool to restore pixels to their original state:

6 Use the Mirror tool to copy pixels into the brush area. The tool reflects the area perpendicular to the direction of the stroke.

7 Use the Push Left tool to move pixels to the left when you drag upward, to the right when you drag downward.

Pattern Maker

Use the Pattern Maker plug-in to generate patterns based on a selected area of an image. You can create and preview multiple pattern variations until you find one you like.

1 Open an image that will provide the sample pixels for the pattern. Choose Filter>Pattern Maker.

2 Use the Selection tool to create a selection which will form the basis of the pattern.

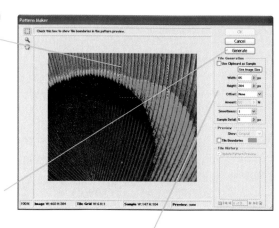

You cannot make a pattern from a non-rectangular selection.

3 Click the Generate button to preview the results.

4 Experiment with settings in the Tile Generation area of the dialog box. Then click the Generate button again. Repeat the process as required.

Work with a copy of an image when using the Pattern Maker: when you OK the dialog box, the new pattern tiles fill the image window.

5 Use the Tile History controls to move backward and forward through the patterns you have generated.

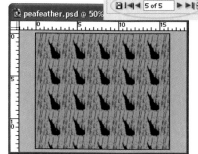

6 OK the dialog box when you have created a pattern you want to utilize.

Filter Gallery

The Filter Gallery allows you to preview and apply individual or multiple filter effects to an entire image, a layer or a selection.

The Filter Gallery is not available for images in CMYK color mode.

1 To show the Filter Gallery, choose Filter>Filter Gallery. A preview of the image with the currently selected filter appears on the left of the window.

Not all Photoshop filters are available from within the Filter Gallery.

2 Click the Reveal/Hide triangle for each filter category to show or hide the filters available for that category.

3 Click a filter thumbnail to apply it to the preview. Use the individual controls on the right hand side of the window to experiment and create the settings you want to use. Each filter effect has its own, specific set of controls.

4 In the Preview area, use the "-" or "+" buttons, or the zoom pop-up to zoom in or out on an area of the preview. Position your cursor in the preview area, then click and drag to reposition the preview.

5 Use the Reveal/Hide button (⏶) to hide the filter thumbnails area to create a larger preview area if necessary. You can choose filters from the Filter drop down menu if you hide the thumbnails.

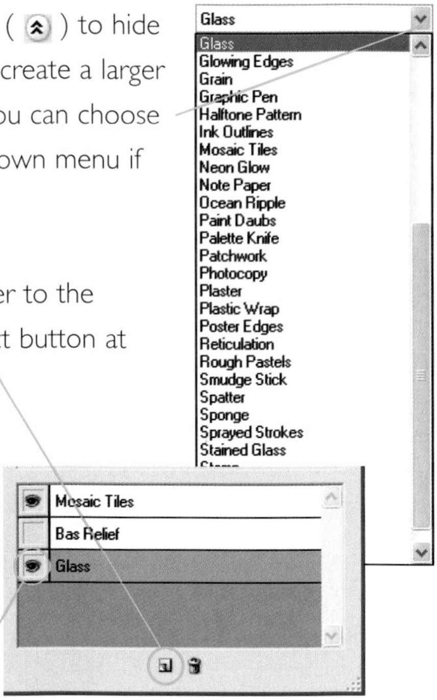

Glass

Glass
Glowing Edges
Grain
Graphic Pen
Halftone Pattern
Ink Outlines
Mosaic Tiles
Neon Glow
Note Paper
Ocean Ripple
Paint Daubs
Palette Knife
Patchwork
Photocopy
Plaster
Plastic Wrap
Poster Edges
Reticulation
Rough Pastels
Smudge Stick
Spatter
Sponge
Sprayed Strokes
Stained Glass

6 To apply more than one filter to the preview, click the New Effect button at the bottom of the window, then click on another filter effect thumbnail. The new filter is added to the bottom of the filter effect list.

Mosaic Tiles

Bas Relief

Glass

7 In the Filter effect list area, click the Eye icon box to apply or hide the filter effect. Drag the filter effect upward or downward to change the order in which the filters are applied. Drag a filter effect into the Wastebasket to remove it.

Web and Multimedia Images

The success of the World Wide Web is in no small part due to its ability to include images in HTML pages. This section looks at some of the considerations for using different image types effectively in formats suited to the environment of the WWW. It also covers techniques for using images in multimedia work.

Balancing file size and image quality is a primary concern when creating images for Web and multimedia use. Generally, the smaller the file size, the quicker the image will load and display on screen. The following techniques examine ways of reducing file size without losing too much image quality.

An image resolution of 72 ppi is usually satisfactory for images intended for screen-based presentations.

Covers

Chapter Fifteen

Save for Web

You can use the keyboard shortcut (Ctrl/ Command+Alt/ option+Shift+S) to go into the Save for Web dialog box.

The Save for Web command offers comprehensive controls for saving images to be used on the World Wide Web. Use the Save for Web command when you want to create an image that is as small as possible – to ensure the fastest possible download times – without sacrificing too much quality.

1 Choose File>Save to save any changes you have made to the image in the current file format. Then choose File>Save for Web.

Use the Zoom and Hand tools to change the magnification and to scroll through images in the preview panes:

2 In the Save for Web dialog box, click the 2-Up tab to compare the original image and the image with optimization settings applied. Click the Original tab to view only the original Photoshop image. Click the Optimized tab to view the image with optimization settings applied. When viewing 2-Up and 4-Up, each optimized pane indicates file format, size, and approximate download time for a specific modem speed in the annotations area.

3 In 2-Up or 4-Up view, make sure the Optimized pane is selected – indicated by a blue border. In the Optimize panel, choose an optimization level from the presets in the Settings pop-up. The Optimized image pane updates so that you can evaluate different options.

GIF, JPEG and PNG file formats are discussed later in this chapter.

4 In 4-Up view, choose Repopulate Views from the Optimization pop-up to update the remaining panes with lower quality optimization settings.

...cont'd

5 Use the Preview menu to change the download time readout to that expected for a particular modem speed. The readout updates accordingly in the annotation area of the optimized preview panes.

Optimization: 4-Up View

The 4-Up tab is particularly useful because it allows you to preview images using a variety of optimization levels before you decide which level of optimization you want.

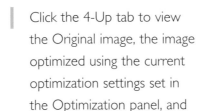

The arrangement of the 4-Up panes varies according to the size of the Save for Web dialog box and the dimensions and orientation of the image.

1 Click the 4-Up tab to view the Original image, the image optimized using the current optimization settings set in the Optimization panel, and two lower quality variations of the current optimization settings.

To return an optimized version of the image to its original state, select the Optimized pane, then choose Original from the bottom of the Optimization Settings pop-up menu:

2 To use one of the lower quality comparison panes as the Optimized image, click inside one of the panes to select it. A blue highlight border on the pane indicates that it is selected. Choose Repopulate Views from the Optimization panel pop-up. The selected pane becomes the Optimized image. Its optimization settings appear in the Optimization area. The comparison panes update with lower quality optimization settings.

For an image that contains slices, click the Slices Visibility button to view the slices in the Save for Web dialog box:

3 To compare different, unrelated optimization settings, click on a comparison pane to select it, then choose an optimization setting from the Settings pop-up. In this case, make sure you do not use the Repopulate Views command.

Preview & Save Optimized Images

You can preview an optimized image in a Web browser before you make a final decision on which optimization settings to save. This can be a useful check before committing yourself to saving the file.

Choose a browser from the Browser Preview pop-up from the bottom of the dialog box. The browser launches and displays the image from the selected pane. Image details such as file format, dimensions and file size are listed below the image. Below the image details is the HTML code necessary to display the image.

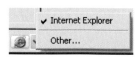

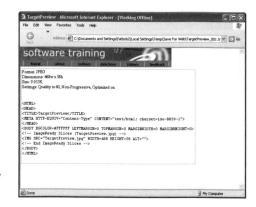

To save an optimized image, select the pane with the settings you want to use. Click Save in the Save for Web dialog box.

Use standard Macintosh/Windows techniques to navigate to the folder in which you want to save the image. Enter a file name for the image. The file extension for the optimization settings is automatically appended to the file name. Make sure you don't delete it. The file is saved using the current settings in the Optimize panel.

4 Select HTML and Images from the Save as Type pop-up menu, to generate the HTML code necessary to display the image as a separate file. This file is automatically named and saved in the same folder as the optimized image. The

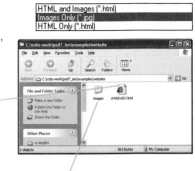

optimized image is saved in an images folder which Photoshop creates automatically within the folder you specify.

5 To specify whether the HTML file uses a table, or Cascading Style Sheets to display an image with slices, choose Other from the Settings pop-up menu. Choose Slices from the pop-up menu. Create the settings you require in the Slice Output area of the Output Settings dialog box.

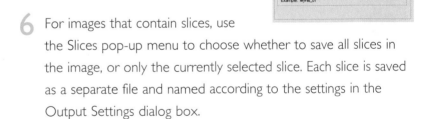

6 For images that contain slices, use the Slices pop-up menu to choose whether to save all slices in the image, or only the currently selected slice. Each slice is saved as a separate file and named according to the settings in the Output Settings dialog box.

7 To change the way in which slices are named, in the Output Settings dialog box choose Saving Files from the pop-up menu. Use the File Naming pop-ups to make changes.

GIF Optimization Settings

The GIF file format usually provides the most efficient and flexible optimization controls for images which have areas of flat color, with sharp edges and type, as you often find in logos and buttons.

1 To optimize an image using GIF file format, select the image pane for which you want to create the settings. To create a setting for a slice, use the Slice Select tool to select a slice.

You cannot use the Lossy option with the Interlaced option, or with a Noise or Pattern dither.

2 Choose one of the preset GIF settings from the Settings pop-up menu. Or, to create custom GIF settings, choose GIF from the Format pop-up, then specify settings using the options in the palette.

3 Drag the pop-up Lossy slider or enter a value to reduce file size by discarding color information. Values of 5–10 can often be applied without noticeably degrading the image quality. Choose a color palette (see pages 200–201) and a dither method (see page 202).

Avoid using GIF format if your image contains a gradient. Use JPEG format instead (see page 197).

4 Use the Colors pop-up menu to specify the maximum number of colors in the Color palette. Increase the Web Snap setting to shift colors to their closest Web palette equivalents to help avoid dithering in a browser.

The Interlaced option creates an image that first downloads as a low-resolution preview whilst the full file information is downloaded.

5 Select Transparency to preserve any transparent areas in the image. You can choose a Matte color if you want to blend the edges of transparent areas into the background of a Web page. Use the Transparency pop-up to choose a dither type for the blended areas if required.

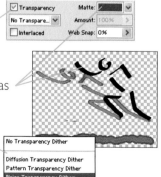

JPEG Optimization Settings

JPEG optimization works best on continuous-tone images such as photographs. JPEG compression can preserve more detail in photographic-type images than GIF and still provide considerable file size reduction.

JPEG compression is "lossy". In order to make the file size of an image smaller, some image data is discarded, reducing the quality of the image.

1 To optimize an image using JPEG file format, select the image pane for which you want to create the settings. To create a setting for a slice, use the Slice Select tool to select a slice.

2 Choose one of the preset JPEG settings from the Settings pop-up menu. Or, to create custom JPEG settings, choose JPEG from the format pop-up, then specify settings using the options in the palette.

3 Use the Quality pop-up to choose a quality setting, or drag the pop-up Quality slider. Use a high setting to preserve most detail in the image with a larger file size. Reduce the quality setting to achieve greater compression and a smaller file size but with reduced image quality.

For medium to high JPEG compression settings, you can use a small Blur value, e.g. 0.1 to 0.5 to blur pattern artifacts that may appear along sharp edges. Higher values may reduce image detail noticeably.

4 Select Optimized to create JPEGs with a slightly smaller file size. Some older browsers do not recognize this setting. Choose Progressive to cause the image to download to the browser in a number of passes, each pass building more detail into the image until it has downloaded completely. Use Blur settings, if required, to allow greater compression on the file. Settings of less than 0.5 are recommended.

5 JPEG compression does not support transparency in images. You can fill transparent areas with a Matte color to simulate transparency, provided you know the background color against which the image will be viewed.

PNG File Format

PNG is a relatively new file format for saving images for use on the Web. There are 2 PNG file format options: PNG-8 and PNG-24.

As a relatively new image file format, not all browsers, especially older browsers, can display images in PNG format.

PNG-8

PNG-8 file format uses 8-bit color which allows a maximum of 256 colors in an image. It is most effective at compressing areas of solid, flat color, typically found in line art, logos and illustrations with type.

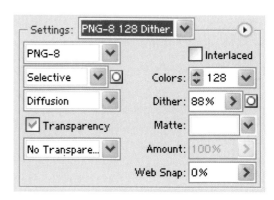

PNG-8 is a lossless compression formula – no color information is lost during compression. Depending on the image, PNG-8 compression can produce files 10–30% smaller than the same image compressed using GIF format.

For images which use a very limited range of colors, the GIF format can produce smaller file sizes than PNG-8. Use the 4-Up tab when saving images to choose the best optimization level.

PNG-8 file format can support background transparency and background matting. Background matting enables you to blend the edges of an image into the background color you set as the background color of your Web page.

PNG-24

PNG-24 supports 24-bit color which allows millions of colors in the image. Like JPEG, this is a good format when you want to preserve subtle transitions in tone and color in a photographic type image.

Multilevel transparency is not supported by all browsers.

PNG-24 uses a lossless compression formula – no color information is discarded during compression. As a result, PNG-24 file sizes are typically larger than if you save the image using JPEG file format.

PNG-24 supports background transparency and background matting. PNG-24 also supports multilevel transparency which allows greater control over the way in which an image blends into the background color of a Web page.

Indexed Color Mode

You can convert RGB or Grayscale images to Indexed Color mode.

Indexed Color mode is an important factor in the preparation of images for use on the World Wide Web and in multimedia applications. It provides an efficient method for reducing the size of a color image. When you work on RGB color images in Photoshop, these are typically 24-bit images, capable of displaying over 16 million colors. Indexed Color Mode converts images to single channel, 8-bit images, capable of displaying a maximum of 256 colors.

Make a selection before you convert to Indexed Color mode, to weight the color table towards the colors that occur in the selection.

1 To convert an RGB color image to Indexed Color mode, choose Image>Mode> Indexed Color.

2 Use the Palette pop-up to specify a color palette which controls and limits the colors that will be used in the image. (See the next page.)

For Uniform, Perceptual, Selective and Adaptive color palettes you can set an exact number of colors to include. Enter a value below 256.

3 Choose an option from the Forced pop-up to force the inclusion of certain colors in the color table.

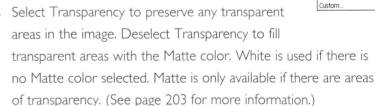

When you save a file with an image preview, you increase the size of the file. To save files without a preview, select Edit>Preferences>File Handling>Never Save (in the Image Previews pop-up menu).

4 Select Transparency to preserve any transparent areas in the image. Deselect Transparency to fill transparent areas with the Matte color. White is used if there is no Matte color selected. Matte is only available if there are areas of transparency. (See page 203 for more information.)

5 Set dithering options. (See page 202).

Color Palettes

When working with GIF compression settings you can also choose color palettes from the Palette pop-up in the Optimize area of the Save for Web dialog box in Photoshop and the Optimize Palette in ImageReady.

A color palette controls the 256 possible colors that exist in an Indexed Color or GIF image. Photoshop/ImageReady uses three methods for creating color tables in images: dynamic, fixed and custom.

Dynamic – Perceptual, Selective and Adaptive color palettes are created dynamically. Each time you optimize the image, the palette created is based on the colors occurring in the image. Different images will generate different palettes.

Fixed – the Web, Mac OS, Windows, Black & White and Grayscale color palettes are fixed. There is a limited, or fixed range of colors. If your optimization settings specify fewer than 256 colors, this reduced range of colors is drawn from the fixed color table.

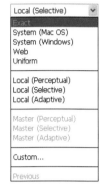

Custom – Custom palettes use colors created or modified by the user. Existing GIF and PNG-8 files also have custom palettes.

System palettes

This is the standard, 8-bit system palette of either the Macintosh or Windows system.

Local color palettes are based on colors present in the active image. Master color palettes are based on a master color palette created in ImageReady.

Exact

If the image you are converting already has fewer than 256 colors, Exact is the default. The actual number of colors is indicated in the Colors entry box. You cannot dither an Exact palette.

Web

This is a palette reduced to 216 or fewer colors. Use this palette to achieve consistency across different platforms and when you want to use more than one image on the same Web page. Images which are based on different color palettes can look artificial when seen side by side.

Uniform

This palette is based on a uniform sampling of colors from the color spectrum.

Adaptive

This palette is built around the colors that actually occur in an image. For individual images, it gives better results than Web, as the color table is created by sampling colors from the most frequently occurring areas of the color spectrum in the image.

Custom

This option takes you into the Color Table dialog box and allows you to create your own custom color table.

Previous

Previous is only available after you have converted an image using Adaptive or Custom methods. It uses exactly the same palette as created by the previous conversion.

Perceptual

The Perceptual option creates a color palette biased towards colors to which the human eye is most sensitive.

Selective

This is similar to Perceptual, but biased towards broad areas of color in the image and also the preservation of Web colors. Selective is the default.

You can specify an exact number of colors for an Indexed Color image if you don't want the maximum 256 steps. Enter a value in the Colors field.

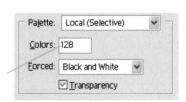

Dithering

Dithering is a technique that simulates colors that are not actually in the color palette. On computer monitors that support only 256 colors, dithering takes place to simulate a greater range of colors in an image than the monitor is actually capable of displaying. For Web images this is referred to as browser dither. Dithering juxtaposes pixels of different colors to create the illusion of additional colors.

Dithering is not recommended for JPEG images.

To minimize the occurrence of browser dither, create the image using only Web-safe colors.

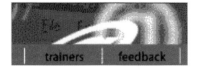

Choose a dithering method for an image when you optimize it. This is referred to as application dither – the dither is built into the image.

Images with areas of solid color may compress best with Dither set to None. Images with gradients usually need dithering to prevent obvious banding.

For GIF images, in the Save for Web dialog box, choose an option from the Dither pop-up. For Diffusion, set a Dither Amount. Higher values result in more dithering which creates the appearance of a greater number of colors in the image. Higher values can also increase the file size, depending on the image.

No Dither
No dithering is applied to the image.

Pattern
This creates a square dither pattern, similar to halftones, to simulate colors not available in the color table.

Diffusion
The results of Diffusion are usually less noticeable than Pattern as the dithering is spread across a range of pixels.

Noise
Applies a random dither pattern. This option can be used for images with slices.

Save As JPEG

For a general introduction to the JPEG format, see page 47.

JPEG is a compression format, widely used for preparing images for the World Wide Web. Use JPEG when you are working with photographic-type images, and when preserving color detail and quality in the image are more important than download time considerations. JPEG does not allow transparency, and file sizes may be larger than for images exported in GIF format, depending on the compression level you choose.

1 To save an image in JPEG format, choose File>Save As. Specify a location, enter a name, then choose JPEG from the Formats pop-up. OK the dialog box.

Save images with gradients in the JPEG format, as the JPEG format produces smaller file sizes than GIFs with an Adaptive palette.

2 Choose a color from the Matte pop-up to simulate background transparency in the image. You need to know the background color of the Web page, in order to match the matte color to it.

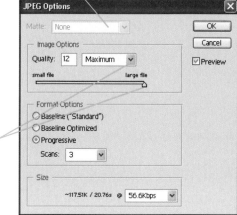

JPEG is most suited to compressing continuous-tone images (images in which the distinction between immediately neighboring pixels is slight). JPEG is not the best format for saving flat color images.

3 Use the Quality pop-up to specify the amount of compression, or drag the slider. "Maximum" gives best quality, retaining most of the detail in the image, but least compression. "Low" gives lowest image quality, but maximum compression.

4 For Format Options, choose Baseline Optimized to optimize the color quality of the image. Select Progressive and enter a number for Scans to download the image in a series of passes which add detail progressively until the image is completely displayed. Click OK to export the file.

Web Photo Gallery

The Web Photo Gallery command allows you set up a website that features your images, quickly and simply, without the need to write any HTML. The website has a home page with thumbnail image links to other pages with full-size images, and includes navigation buttons.

1 To create a Web Photo Gallery choose File>Automate>Web Photo Gallery.

2 Choose a template to control the look and feel of the website from the Style pop-up menu. A thumbnail of the style appears on the right of the dialog box. Include an e-mail address if you want viewers to be able to contact you via e-mail.

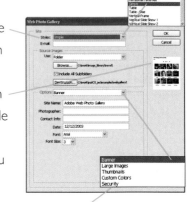

3 In the Options area, use the pop-up menu to specify settings for text labels on the site, and to specify size and compression settings for thumbnail and full-size images.

4 Click the Browse button to navigate to the folder which contains the images you want to include on the website. Click the Destination button to navigate to the folder in which you want Photoshop to create the website. Click OK, then test the Web Photo Gallery in a browser.

Working with ImageReady

With the rapid, commercial development of the World Wide Web since the mid 1990's onward, there has been a growing need for a distinct set of controls and features that allow the user to create eye-catching, optimized images with small file sizes for rapid download times on modems. Creating images for the Web brings a different range of possibilities, technical requirements and constraints when compared with creating images destined to be printed on paper.

ImageReady is designed specifically to meet these rapidly emerging needs. It has dedicated optimization controls and you can create animated GIF files, slices, rollovers and background images.

Covers

Chapter Sixteen

Photoshop and ImageReady

You can work on an image in Photoshop, then continue to make further adjustments to the same image in ImageReady, or vice versa. Use the Edit in ImageReady/ Photoshop button or command to move images seamlessly from one environment to the other so that you can work in the environment that gives you the most control for whatever task you are attempting.

ImageReady and Photoshop exist as separate application environments, yet work side by side with one another. Much of the toolset and many of the palettes and working techniques are identical in both environments. ImageReady is specifically optimized for creating images for the Web and multimedia, whereas Photoshop provides a powerful feature set for creating images for print, but at the same time provides controls for the creation of images destined for the screen.

Moving between applications

1 For an image you've begun to prepare in Photoshop, choose File>Edit in Image Ready. Or click the Edit in ImageReady button.

Many of the ImageReady palettes have the same range of functionality as their counterparts in Photoshop. The Animation, Slice, Image Map and Rollover palettes are available in ImageReady only.

2 Image Ready then launches and the image appears in the ImageReady application window. You can now make further changes to the image in

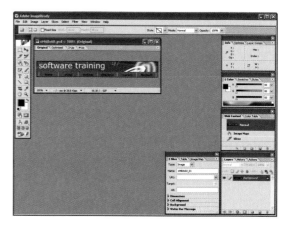

ImageReady. The image moves from the Photoshop application environment to the ImageReady environment.

Individual or multiple changes you make in one application environment are represented in the History palette of the other application as a single entry called "Update from File".

3 To move the image currently active in ImageReady back into the Photoshop working environment again, click the Edit in Photoshop button, or choose File>Edit in Photoshop.

The ImageReady Toolbox & Window

The ImageReady Toolbox is largely the same as the Photoshop Toolbox. This page indicates the tools found in ImageReady which are not found in Photoshop, and indicates how to create Tear-off tool groups.

Image Map tools

Button tools

Some tools, such as the Editing and Toning tools, are found in different locations in the ImageReady toolbox:

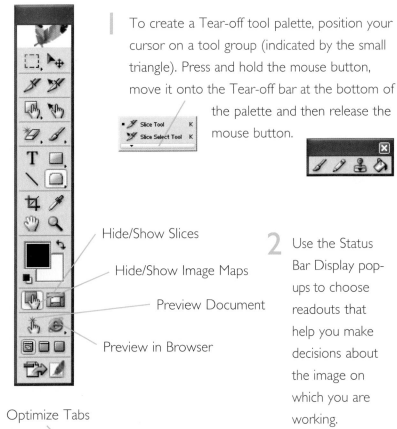

1 To create a Tear-off tool palette, position your cursor on a tool group (indicated by the small triangle). Press and hold the mouse button, move it onto the Tear-off bar at the bottom of the palette and then release the mouse button.

Hide/Show Slices

Hide/Show Image Maps

Preview Document

Preview in Browser

2 Use the Status Bar Display pop-ups to choose readouts that help you make decisions about the image on which you are working.

Optimize Tabs

Status Bar Display pop-up

Creating and Saving Images

Although creating and saving images in ImageReady is very similar to the same routines in Photoshop, there are some differences to be aware of.

In ImageReady's New Document dialog box there is no Color Mode pop-up. Images in ImageReady are always in RGB mode.

1 To create a new file in ImageReady, choose File>New. Enter values in pixels for Width and Height, or use the Size pop-up to choose a preset size. There is no need to give the file a name at this stage.

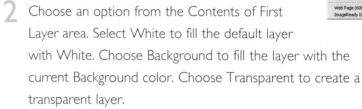

In the ImageReady New Document dialog box you do not set a resolution. The resolution of images in ImageReady is always 72 ppi.

2 Choose an option from the Contents of First Layer area. Select White to fill the default layer with White. Choose Background to fill the layer with the current Background color. Choose Transparent to create a transparent layer.

You work in Photoshop file format (.PSD) as you build and edit an image. Optimize the image when you have finished working on it and want to prepare it for the WWW.

3 To save a file in the first instance, choose File>Save As. In the Save dialog box, specify a location in which you want to save the file. Enter a name. The .PSD file extension is automatically added to the file name. Make sure you retain the file extension. Click the Save button. Continue to work on the file in Photoshop format and use the Save command (Ctrl/Command+S) regularly to save changes you make.

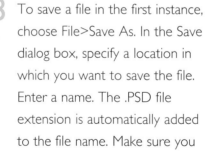

Make sure you are working in the Original tab to edit and change the image.

4 When the image is finished and you want to save an optimized version for use on the World Wide Web or in a multimedia application, use the Save Optimized As command. (See page 214 for information on saving optimized files.)

Handling Type in ImageReady

Type is entered and edited directly in the image window, as it is in Photoshop.

With the Type tool selected, click and drag in the image window to create Paragraph type. (See page 135 for further information.)

1 To enter type, choose the Type tool, position your cursor in the image window, then click to place the text insertion point.

2 Enter type using the keyboard. The type automatically creates a new Type layer in the Layers palette. The new layer is positioned above the previously active layer. Type appears formatted with the current settings in the Type palettes. Select a different layer, or choose a different tool, to continue working with the image.

With the Type tool selected, click the Change Text Orientation button in the Options bar to create vertical type:

3 To make changes to the formatting of type, select the Type tool. Position your cursor carefully on the text or you may find that you create a new type layer accidentally. Drag across the text in the image window. You can highlight type in this way, even if the Type layer is not active. Alternatively, just click on a type layer to make it active if you want to change the formatting for the entire layer.

You should consider using slightly larger type when working with images for the Web than you would for printed images.

4 To change type settings, with the Type tool selected, choose options from the Options bar.

5 Click the Palettes button in the Options bar to display the Character and Paragraph palettes. These palettes offer the full range of controls available in Photoshop and ImageReady. (See pages 137–139 for information on using the Character and Paragraph palettes.)

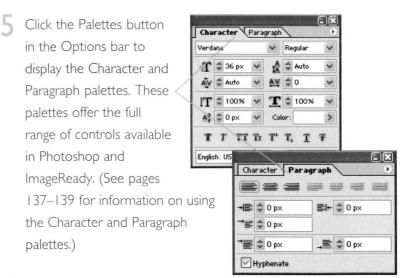

6 When a Type layer is active and when you choose any tool other than the Type tool, the type highlights with a blue line running across the base of the type and a small square indicates the current alignment setting for the type.

7 To reposition type, make sure the Type layer is active, select the Move tool ( ), then drag the type. As you reposition a type layer, or any other layer in ImageReady, alignment guides appear as you drag. Use these interactive alignment guides to align the contents of layers accurately.

8 With a type layer selected, select the Show Transform Box to display a transformation bounding box around the type. Drag a handle to transform the type visually. (See page 128 for further information on transforming layers.)

The Shape Tools

Alignment guides appear as you draw and move shapes in an image with multiple layers, provided that Snap is selected in the View menu and Smart Guides is selected in the View>Show sub-menu. Use these interactive alignment guides to align contents on different layers accurately.

Use the Rectangle, Rounded Rectangle, Ellipse, Line and Button Shape tools to create either a New Shape layer, or a Filled shape. The techniques for using each tool are the same.

1. To draw a rectangle, oval, line or button shape choose the appropriate tool. Select either the Create New Shape layer button or the Create Filled Region button.

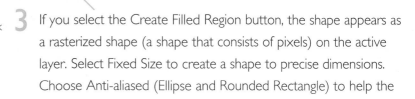

There is no Direct Selection tool in ImageReady. If you want to edit the vector path of a Shape layer, jump to Adobe Photoshop.

2. If you select the Create New Shape layer button, use the Options bar to create settings for the Shape layer. You can use the Style pop-up to apply a pre-defined Layer Style to a Shape layer. When you drag in the image window the shape automatically creates a new layer.

To move or transform a Shape layer, click on the Shape layer icon in the Layers palette:

Select the Move tool and a transform bounding box appears around the shape:

(See page 128 for information on transforming layers.)

3. If you select the Create Filled Region button, the shape appears as a rasterized shape (a shape that consists of pixels) on the active layer. Select Fixed Size to create a shape to precise dimensions. Choose Anti-aliased (Ellipse and Rounded Rectangle) to help the object blend into its background by creating a slightly soft edge.

4. Position your cursor in the image window, then press and drag to create the shape. Release the mouse when the object is the required size. The object fills with the current foreground color.

5. To create a square or a circle, hold down Shift and drag with the Shape tool. Start to drag with a Shape tool, then hold down Alt/option, to draw a shape from the center out.

The ImageReady Optimize Palette

The basic principles for optimizing images in ImageReady are the same as in Photoshop's Save for Web dialog box (see pages 192–193). The main difference is that the Original, Optimized, 2-Up and 4-Up tabs are part of the ImageReady window and therefore always available. The optimization settings and controls are located in the Optimize palette.

The purpose of optimizing an image is to create an acceptable balance between image quality and download times.

1   Choose Window>Optimize if the Optimize palette is not already showing.

2   Use the Preset pop-up menu to choose one of the pre-defined optimization settings. The Optimized image pane updates according to the settings you choose.

When you choose new optimization settings for the Optimized image pane, the remaining panes in 4-Up view do not update automatically. Choose Repopulate Views from the Optimize palette menu to repopulate the other panes with lower quality versions of those in the Optimized pane.

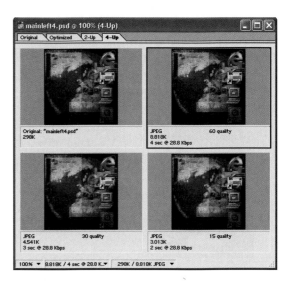

3   Use the 2-Up and 4-Up tabs to compare the visual quality of different optimization settings, along with file format, file size and download time readouts. To hide or show annotations in the 2-Up/4-Up views, choose View>Hide/Show Optimization Info.

4 In 4-Up view, select an optimized version of the image – a black highlight border appears around the selected pane. Choose Repopulate Views from the pop-up menu in the Optimize palette. The selected version now becomes the Optimized version and ImageReady automatically generates two smaller, lower-quality versions of the optimized image in the two remaining panes.

When you want to create custom optimization settings, click the expand/collapse triangle for Color Table, Dither, Transparency, Options (GIF and PNG-8), or Quality, Transparency, Options (JPEG and PNG-24). See pages 196–198 for further information on the options available:

5 When you begin working with optimization settings, use the pre-defined settings in the Preset pop-up as the basis for optimizing images.

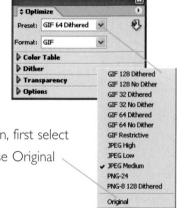

6 To restore an optimized version of the image to the original version, first select the optimized version, then choose Original from the Preset pop-up menu.

7 If optimizing an image to a specific file size is more important than the resultant image quality, choose Optimize to File Size from the Optimize palette pop-up menu. Enter the required file size. Select the Auto Select GIF/JPEG option to allow ImageReady to choose the most effective compression format. Choose Current settings to use the current format as the basis for reducing the file size.

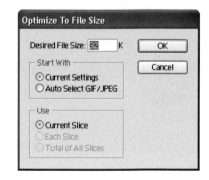

Saving an Optimized Image

After you decide on optimization settings that give you the correct balance between image quality and file size, you can then save an optimized version of the file.

1 If you are working with the Optimized tab selected, check that the current optimization settings in the Optimize palette are the ones you want. Then choose File>Save Optimized As.

If you are working on an optimized image in 2-Up or 4-Up view, when you choose File>Save Optimized As, the settings you apply to the image are those for the selected image pane.

2 If you are working in 2-Up view, make sure the Optimized pane is selected. If you are working with the 4-Up tab, make sure you select the pane with the settings you want to use for optimizing the

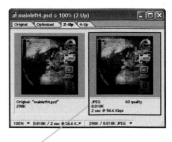

image. A selected pane is indicated by a black highlight border. Then choose File>Save Optimized As.

3 In the Save Optimized dialog box, specify a location and name for the file. The file format extension (e.g. .gif) is appended automatically. Make sure you retain the file extension.

4 For the Save as Type pop-up menu, leave the Save Images option selected. Select

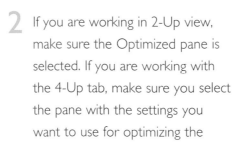

the HTML and Images option if you want to save an additional HTML file that includes the image name, its dimensions in pixels and any other code necessary to display the image on a Web page. The HTML file is saved as a separate file with a .html extension in the

Select Save Selected Slices from the Slices pop-up menu only when you have selected specific slices in the image prior to choosing the Save Optimized As command. ImageReady creates a complete HTML table capable of displaying the selected slices.

specified folder. The image file is saved in an images folder that ImageReady creates automatically within the specified folder. This option is useful when saving images with slices (see Chapter 18.) Click the Save button.

Animations and Rollovers

Animations are built from a series of GIF images which, when displayed in quick succession, create the illusion of movement. You create and control animations using the Animation and Layers palettes in ImageReady. Animations can be saved in GIF file format or exported to Macromedia® Flash™ (SWF) format.

A rollover is an effect that is triggered by a mouse action. For example, a button may glow when the mouse cursor moves over it and then change shape in response to a mouse click.

Animations and rollovers can bring impact, movement and variety to a Web page, but they can also become distracting if not used carefully. Use these effects when they bring dynamism to a page and contribute to the message and content. Don't use animations and rollovers for their own sake.

Covers

Chapter Seventeen

Creating a Simple Animation

Animations can range from the very simple to the very complex. Try to keep your animations simple at the outset. Remember that animation effects, if used indiscriminately on Web pages, can be distracting and as a result lose their intended impact.

When you open or create an image in ImageReady, the image becomes the first frame in the Animation palette by default, even if you do not intend to create an animation.

1 Create an image in Photoshop, or directly in ImageReady as in this example. Use layers as the basis for the animation. The layers you create form the basic building blocks for the animation. Put elements you want to animate on separate layers.

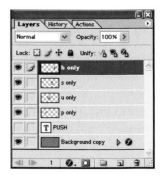

To avoid confusion as you create an animation, make sure that you have created and finished editing all the objects and layers you want to use, before you start to build the animation.

2 Hide any layers containing elements you do not want to appear at the start of the animation.

3 Choose Window >Animation to show the Animation palette if it is not already showing. Choose New Frame from the palette's pop-up menu, or click the New Frame button. This creates frame 2, which is a duplicate of the preceding frame.

Choose Window> Workspace> Interactivity Palette Locations to create a convenient arrangement of palettes for building animations and other web effects.

Animations are saved in the GIF file format. The JPEG and PNG formats cannot be used for animations.

When working in ImageReady, it is best to create and edit the animation in Original view. Options for editing animations are more limited in Optimized view.

Any changes you make on a layer that affect actual pixel values – for example, painting, changing color or tone, or using transform commands – will affect all frames in the animation in which the layer is present.

4 Make a change to a layer. Changes you make to the layers, such as layer visibility, position, opacity or layer effects, form the animation when the frames are viewed in quick succession. In this example the "P" is moved next to the "U".

5 Repeat Steps 3–4 as necessary. In this example, both the "P" and "U" are moved to the "S". Then, for the final frame, the "P", "U" and "S" are moved up to the "H".

6 Save the animation in Photoshop format as you build and make changes. This means you can return to the original file, if necessary, to make further adjustments. (See page 220 for information on saving an optimized version of the animation for use on the Web.)

Playing and Managing Frames

As you build an animation you will need to preview it and to control aspects such as looping and frame rate.

To play an animation, click the Play button. The animation plays in the image window and each frame in the Animation palette highlights in sequence as the animation plays. Click the Stop button to stop the animation at the current frame.

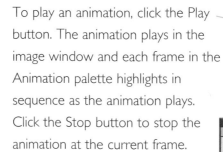

To select multiple, consecutive frames, click on the first frame, hold down Shift, then click on the last frame in the range you want to select.

To select nonconsecutive frames, click on a frame to select it, hold down Ctrl/ Command, then click on other frames to add them to the previously selected frame.

To select a frame, click on the frame in the Animation palette. The frame highlights and becomes the current frame. The current frame is displayed in the image window. It is the frame that can currently be edited.

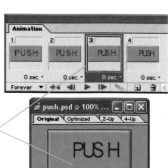

To delete a frame, first click on it to select it. Then click the Wastebasket button at the bottom of the palette. Alternatively, drag the frame into the Wastebasket, or choose Delete Frame from the palette menu.

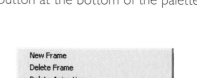

New Frame
Delete Frame
Delete Animation

When you select multiple frames, you can distinguish the current frame by the black highlight border around the frame.

To change the position of a frame, select the frame you want to move, then drag it to a new location. Release the mouse when you see a thick black bar at the position to which you want to move the frame.

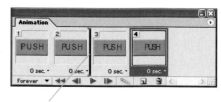

5 To set the frame delay rate (the speed at which frames advance), first select a frame or multiple frames. Use the Frame Delay pop-up located below each frame. Either choose a value from the preset list, or choose Other then specify a delay in the Set Frame Delay dialog box.

Preview animations in a browser working live over the internet to get an accurate idea of the delay you specify.

6 To specify looping options, use the Loop pop-up in the bottom left corner of the Animation palette. Forever plays the animation in a continuous loop. Choose Other to specify a set number of times you want the animation to play. Enter a value in the Play ... times field.

Copying and pasting frames

You can copy a frame or multiple frames and then paste the copied frame(s) into a new location in the current animation, or into a completely different animation.

1 To copy a frame, first select the frame. A black highlight indicates the frame is selected. Choose Copy Frame from the Animation palette menu.

2 Select a frame in which you want to paste the copied frame. Choose Paste Frame from the Animation palette menu. Choose an option for Paste Method then click OK.

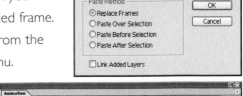

Optimizing and Saving Animations

When you have created the frames for your animation and you are satisfied with the effect, you can optimize and then save the animation.

Continue to test other optimization settings and preview them until you are satisfied with the results.

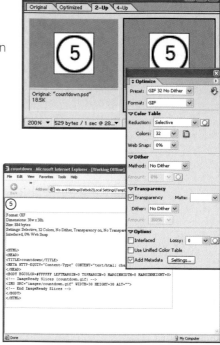

1 To optimize an animation, click the Optimize tab in the ImageReady window. In the Optimize palette, choose the optimization settings you want to use from the Settings pop-up.

2 To preview the results of the optimization settings, choose File>Preview in, then choose from the list of available browsers. The browser launches and the animation plays in the browser window.

File format information and HTML code are displayed below the animation for information purposes. Close the browser.

To export an animation to Flash (SWF) format, choose File>Export> Macromedia Flash (SWF). For a simple animation accept the default settings in the export dialog box, or create custom settings:

OK the dialog box. Specify a location and name for the file. Open the animation in a browser to preview the result. ImageReady converts animation frames to SWF animation frames, but slice, image map and rollover settings are discarded.

3 To save the animation, choose File>Save Optimized As. Specify a location and a name for the file. Make sure you retain the .GIF file extension which should appear automatically.

4 Select the Save HTML file option to save the HTML code for the animation file. The HTML file is saved in the same folder and with the same name as the animation, but with a HTML file extension. Make sure you leave the Save Images option selected. Click the Save button.

Tweening

In ImageReady, the Tween command allows you to create smoother animations quickly and easily, by automatically creating additional frames between existing frames in the animation. These additional, in-between frames create smoother movement in the animation.

The term "tweening" is derived from a traditional animation term "in betweening" where additional frames were created between key frames to create smooth animation effects.

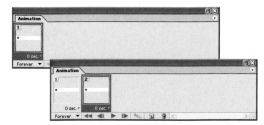

1 To tween a frame, first click the New Frame button to create a duplicate of the first frame.

2 Make a change (for example, reposition an object) to the layer on which you are working.

Use tweening to dramatically reduce the amount of time needed to create smooth animations.

3 Click the Tween button in the Animations palette, or choose Tween from the palette pop-up menu.

Tweened animation frames do not require a new layer for each new frame. The tweening effect takes place on an individual layer.

4 For Layers, select the Selected Layer option to vary only the currently selected layer in the selected frame, otherwise leave the option set to All Layers.

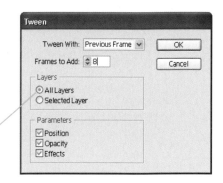

You can tween the last and first frames in an animation. This is useful to create a smooth transition from the end of an animation back to the beginning, when the animation is designed to loop a number of times.

5 Choose Parameter options to specify which elements you want to tween. In this example it is important to choose Position, as it is the position of the layers in the animation that

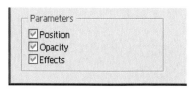

varies. Select Opacity if opacity settings vary between frames. Select Effects if Layer Effects vary between frames.

6 Use the Tween with: pop-up to choose the frame with which you want to tween the currently selected frame.

7 Enter a value in the Frames to Add: field to specify the number of in-between frames. The more in-between frames you add, the smoother the animation, but the result is a larger file size.

8 OK the dialog box. The in-between frames are added as new frames. Subsequent frames are renumbered accordingly.

Creating a Simple Rollover

A rollover image can have a number of different states. The "Normal" state is the appearance of the image when it first loads in the browser window. The "Over" state is the state of the image when the mouse cursor moves over it.

A layer-based slice is indicated by a slice icon in the layers palette entry for that layer:

When you save an image with rollover states, each state is saved as a separate image. When you save the image with HTML coding, ImageReady automatically creates the JavaScript code necessary to display the rollover effects in a browser.

If you find the display of slices in the image window disconcerting, click the Slice Visibility button in the Toolbox:

A rollover image is an image whose appearance changes according to various mouse actions. For example, the image may change when the mouse cursor moves over it, or when it is clicked by the mouse. Rollover images are commonly used on Web pages and in multimedia interfaces. You use the Web Content palette together with the Layers palette to create rollover states for an image.

1 Create the layers and any layer styles you will need for the rollover states in your image. Before you begin to build the rollover states, make sure you show only those layers that you want to be visible in the Normal state of the image.

2 In the Layers palette, select the layer whose contents you want to use to trigger the rollover effect.

3 In the Web Content palette, click the Create Layer-based Rollover button, or choose Create Layer-based rollover from the palette menu. This creates a layer-based slice for the contents of the selected layer and automatically creates the first rollover state — the Over state — as an entry below the layer-based slice entry.

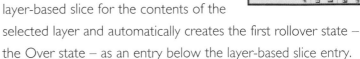

4 Slices appear in the image window and a Slice tool icon (✂) appears on the selected layer to indicate it is a layer-based slice.

5 Make sure you keep the Over state selected. Make changes to the Layers palette to represent the Over state of the image. This is the version of the image you want the viewer to see when they roll their cursor over the image. In this example, an outer glow is added to the contents of the layer.

Remember to click the Preview Document button to return to normal image editing mode when you have finished testing the rollover.

6 To check the result, click on the Normal and Over state entries in the Rollover palette in turn to see how the image in the image window changes. Or click the Preview Document button (Y) in the Toolbox, then move your cursor into the image window and over the rollover slices to see how the image responds.

7 To save the rollover for use in a Web page, choose File>Save Optimized As. Specify a folder and enter a name for the file. Choose HTML and Images from the Save As Type pop-up menu. When you click the Save button, ImageReady creates a HTML file together with the necessary JavaScript to display the rollover in a Web page. The individual images that make up the rollover are stored within an images folder within the specified folder.

8 You can open the HTML file in a browser to preview the results.

Slicing and Image Maps

Slicing allows you to create a single, complete image in Photoshop or ImageReady, then subdivide it into specific areas – the slices. ImageReady automatically generates the HTML code for a table that will hold the sliced image, or the code that will display the image using Cascading Style Sheets.

Using slices you can optimize parts of an image differently for different purposes; slices can become buttons and assigned links; and you can also create rollover states for slices. The functionality of slices varies slightly between Photoshop and ImageReady.

Use image maps to define areas of an image as clickable hypertext links in a Web page.

Covers

Chapter Eighteen

Slices from Guides & the Slice Tool

Slices are rectangular areas of an image that become the contents of a single cell in a HTML table, or that can be coded using Cascading Style Sheets. An image in ImageReady initially consists of a single slice by default, comprising the complete image. When you create a new slice, the remainder of the image is automatically divided into further slices.

You can create slices based on ruler guides or selections, or you can create a slice using the Slice tool. This section looks at techniques for creating slices from guides and using the Slice tool.

Slices from guides

When you use the Create Slices from Guides command, ImageReady deletes previously created slices.

To create ruler guides, choose View>Rulers to show rulers along the top and left edge of the image window if they are not already showing. See page 23 for information on creating ruler guides.

Slices you create using the Create Slices from Guides command and using the Slice tool are created as User-slices.

1 Create or open an image. Drag in ruler guides to indicate where you want to create slices. (See page 23 for information on creating ruler guides.) Click the Edit in ImageReady button if you are not already working in ImageReady.

2 Choose Slices> Create Slices from Guides. The slices appear in the image. Each slice is numbered. Slices created from guides are User-slices. (See page 229 for information on User- and Auto-slices.) A color adjustment, visible when slices are showing, is applied to slices to indicate User- and Auto-slices. (See page 229 for further information.)

Slices are rectangular areas of an image that become the contents of individual cells in a HTML table. When loaded in a browser, the image appears to be a single, composite image. In HTML terms, it is split into discreet, separate areas.

As soon as you select the Slice tool, existing slices display automatically.

"Smart" alignment guides appear as you draw and move slices in an image with multiple layers and/ or existing slices, provided that Snap is selected in the View menu and Smart Guides is selected in the View>Show sub-menu. Use these interactive alignment guides to align slices accurately.

3 Choose the Slice Select tool (O), then click on a slice to select it. A colored bounding box appears around the slice, defining the area of the slice.

4 The selected slice also appears in the Slice palette. Choose Window>Slice if the palette is not already showing. Also, each slice in the image creates an entry in the Web Content palette.

The Slice tool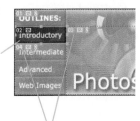

1 To create a slice using the Slice tool, click on the tool to select it. Position your cursor on the image, then drag to define the area of the slice. The slice you define is a User-slice.

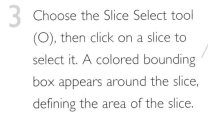

2 When you release the mouse, ImageReady automatically generates additional slices to enable the image to fit into a HTML table. The additional slices are Auto-slices.

3 Hold down Shift as you drag with the Slice tool for a square slice. Hold down Alt/option and drag to create a slice from the center out.

4 Choose View>Snap to>Slices if you want the Slice tool to snap to other slices or guides. The snap takes effect when your cursor comes within 4 pixels of a slice or guide.

Creating Slices from Selections

You can also create slices from selections.

1 Create a selection. Choose Select>Create Slice from Selection. The selection becomes a User-slice. (See page 229 for information on User and Auto-slices.) The User-slice is numbered and the remainder of the image is divided into further slices as necessary to fit the complete image into a HTML table, or for coding as Cascading Style Sheets. The User-slice is selected and a highlight bounding box appears around it. A color adjustment is applied to the remainder of the image. This color adjustment is helpful in distinguishing between User- and Auto-slices.

2 Continue creating slices as necessary. As you create additional slices, slice numbers are updated. Slices are numbered from left to right and top to bottom.

 When you click the Hide Slices button (Q), the color adjustments applied to slices disappears.

 You cannot create slices from selections in Photoshop.

 If you create a slice from a feathered selection, the slice includes the feathered area.

 If you use a non-rectangular selection to create a slice, the slice itself covers a rectangle that encompasses the complete selection.

User- and Auto-slices

It can sometimes be less confusing to hide the display of Auto-slices. Select the Slice-select tool, then click the Hide/Show Auto Slices button in the Options bar.

A slice can have one of two statuses: User or Auto. There are more possibilities for modifying User-slices. Any slices you create (using guides, selections or the Slice tool) are User-slices. Slices created automatically by ImageReady to enable the remainder of the image to fit into a HTML table are Auto-slices. An image in ImageReady automatically consists of one Auto-slice comprising the full image.

You can change or "promote" an Auto-slice into a User-slice. User-slices can be assigned different optimization settings. Auto-slices in an image are initially linked and therefore share the same optimization settings. The link symbol which appears next to Auto-slices indicates that they share the same optimization settings.

You can promote an Auto-slice to a User-slice. In Photoshop select the Promote to User-slice option in the Options bar. In ImageReady choose Slices>Promote to User-slice.

There are two types of slices: Image or No Image. Image slices contain image information – pixels. No Image slices can contain a solid color, or HTML text. An Image slice is identified by the Image icon when slices are visible.

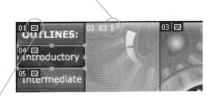

The color adjustment applied to slices dims the brightness and contrast of unselected slices. This is for display purposes only. The color adjustment does not affect the final color of images.

Starting in the top left corner, slices are numbered from left to right and top to bottom. As you add, delete and rearrange slices, slice numbers are updated automatically.

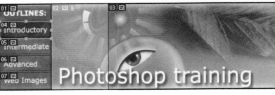

User-slices have blue slice annotation symbols; Auto-slices have gray slice annotation symbols.

User-slices are indicated by a solid boundary line; Auto-slices by a dotted line.

Different color adjustments on User- and Auto-slices and the slice information icons help you distinguish the two statuses. The color adjustment on User-slices is half the strength of the color adjustment used to distinguish Auto-slices.

Working with Slices

Use the following techniques to hide and show slices and to select and deselect slices.

1 To hide slices and slice information such as slice number and slice type icons, click the Hide/Show Slice button (Q) in the Toolbox. To show slices, click the button again (Q).

2 To select a slice, select the Slice Select tool (O). Click on a slice. A colored bounding box with eight selection

handles appears around the slice indicating it is selected. The color adjustment, which defines the area of the slices, is switched off for the selected slice.

3 To select multiple slices, select a slice, hold down Shift then click inside another slice to add it to the selection.

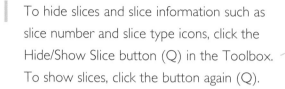

4 When you select a slice, it appears in the Slice palette. Choose Window>Slice to show the Slice palette if it is not already showing. Click the Expand button in the Slice tab, if necessary, to show all option categories for the slice, or click the Expand/Collapse triangle next to individual categories to show/hide specific areas of the palette. The default slice name and slice number appear in the Name entry box. (See page 232 for information on assigning URLs to slices so that they can function as buttons on a Web page.)

Photoshop and ImageReady can generate slices as a HTML table, or as Cascading Style Sheets. In the Save Optimized As dialog box (see page 195), click the Output settings button to specify which method is used.

To delete a User-slice, first select it then press the Backspace or Delete key. Auto-slices are automatically created to fill the same area.

In Photoshop, to hide/show slice numbers, use the Show Slice Numbers option in the Options bar.

You cannot move or resize User-slices in the Photoshop Save for Web dialog box.

To delete all User-slices, in Photoshop choose View>Clear Slices; in ImageReady choose Slices>Delete All.

5 Choose File>Preview in, then select a Browser from the sub-menu to preview the image in the browser window. The automatically generated HTML code

for the sliced image is also displayed in the browser window.

6 Use the Optimize palette to create optimization settings for the image. (See Chapter 16 for details). You can create different optimization settings for individual slices if required.

7 Choose Save Optimized As to save an optimized version of the image. (See page 214 for information on saving optimized images).

8 To move a slice, select the Slice Select tool, position your cursor within the slice you want to move then drag the slice.

9 To resize a slice, select the Slice Select tool. Select a slice then drag a side or corner resize handle.

Assigning URLs to Slices/Image Maps

You can make a slice or image map act as a clickable button that will link to another Web page by assigning a URL to the slice or image map area.

When you assign a URL to an Auto-slice it becomes a User-slice.

1 Select the Slice tool to select a slice. Select the Image Map select tool to select an image map area. Click on a slice or image map to select it. Make sure the Slice or Image Map palette is showing. Details for the selected slice appears in the Slices palette. Information for a selected Image Map area appears in the Image Map palette.

With either the Slice or Slice Selection tool selected, hold down Command/Ctrl to toggle temporarily to the other tool.

2 Slices and Image Map areas are automatically named. An underscore and a slice/image map number are added in the Name field.

3 Enter a URL in the URL entry field. You should include the http:// specifier at the beginning of the URL for absolute paths. You can also specify relative paths. You can choose any previously created URL from the URL pop-up menu.

4 If you are preparing images for a website that uses frames, specify a target frame – where the HTML file you link to will appear – using the Target entry field. Enter the name of the target frame exactly as defined in the frameset file.

Image Maps

The Image Map tools and palette allow you to create areas in an image that become clickable hyperlinks when the image is used in a HTML file. Unlike slicing an image, where individual slices become separate files, creating an image map keeps the image as a single file, with areas of the image defined as links. As well as rectangular areas, image maps enable you to create circular and irregular areas to act as links.

With the Rectangular or Elliptical Image Map tool selected, hold down Shift to create a square or circle.

1 To create an image map, select one of the Image Map tools. Press and drag diagonally to create rectangular or oval image map areas. For the Polygon Image Map tool,

position your cursor on the image, click, move the cursor to a new position (do not click and drag), then click again. Repeat this process to create the shape you require. Click back at the start point to close the shape. You can also double-click to close the shape.

"Smart" alignment guides appear as you draw and move image map areas in an image with multiple layers and/or existing image map areas, provided that Snap is selected in the View menu and Smart Guides is selected in the View>Show sub-menu. Use these interactive alignment guides to align image maps accurately.

2 To show existing image map areas in an image, select the Image Map Select tool, or choose View> Show>Image Maps. You can also click the Image Map Visibility button ( ) in the Toolbox to show/hide image map areas in the image window.

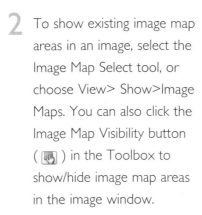

3 Use the Image Map Select tool to select areas of an image map. Click in an image map area to select it.

4 To reposition an image map area, position the Image Map Select tool in the area, then press and drag the area in the image window.

5 To resize a selected image map area, position the Select cursor on one of the resize handles on the area's border, then press and drag.

6 You can also control the size and position of a selected image map area in the Dimensions section of the Image Map palette.

7 To delete an image map area, select it then press the Backspace or Delete key.

Index

H

I

J

L